LEAVING CERTIFICATE

LESS STRESS MORE SUCCESS

English Revision
Ordinary Level

Joseph Kelly

GILL EDUCATION

Gill Education
Hume Avenue
Park West
Dublin 12
www.gilleducation.ie
Gill Education is an imprint of M. H. Gill & Co.

978 0 7171 7567 3
Design by Liz White Designs
Print origination by Carole Lynch

For permission to reproduce photographs, the author and publisher gratefully
acknowledge the following:
© Alamy: 8, 13T, 14, 19, 22, 52, 53, 59, 73, 77, 83, 107, 117R, 143, 151; © Collins: 28, 117L,
117CL; © Dublin City Public Libraries: 69; © Getty Images: 4, 15, 25, 93, 125, 126T, 126B;
© iStock: 13BL, 24, 26, 76, 90, 122; © Rex Features / Shutterstock: 117CR; © Rolling News:
13BR, 148; State Examinations Commission: 1, 5, 111.

For permission to reproduce copyright material the publishers gratefully acknowledge
the following:
Extracts from *The Real Mrs Brown: Brendan O'Carroll*, by Brian Beacom, reproduced by
permission of Hodder and Stoughton Limited. 'A Removal From Terry Street' by Douglas
Dunn (© Douglas Dunn 1968) is printed by permission of United Agents
(www.unitedagents.co.uk) on behalf of Douglas Dunn. Extracts from *Big Maggie* by John B.
Keane, Copyright: © The Estate of John B. Keane, 1988. Reprinted by kind permission of
Mercier Press Ltd., Cork. The article by Michael Palin entitled 'Keeping a Diary' was
reproduced with permission from The Gumby Corporation Ltd.

CONTENTS

Acknowledgements

My sincere thanks to the boys and staff of Naas CBS, who helped with this book in many ways. I must also thank my wonderful parents, as well as my personal editor, Emily-Anne. I hope this book helps in some way to improve the exam results of the many hard-working students out there.

This book is intended to bring confidence to all Leaving Certificate Ordinary Level students preparing for their English exam. With the right attitude and exam-focused knowledge, results will be maximised.

1 Exam Outline and Mental Preparation

- To understand the structure of the exam papers.
- To know the breakdown of marks allocated to each section of the course.
- To develop the right attitude to exam revision.
- To improve crucial reading skills.

Structure of the exam

- Two papers.
- 200 marks each.
- 400 marks in total.

Paper 1

Paper 1 has **two sections:**

Section 1 Comprehending (100 marks)

- **Three reading choices are given,** one of which can be a set of pictures. There will be a common theme to all three texts, although this makes no difference in answering the questions.
- **Read one text and answer the Question A that follows it.** Question A carries 50 marks and is usually broken into three short questions (15 marks + 15 marks + 20 marks).

2017. M.9

Coimisiún na Scrúduithe Stáit
State Examinations Commission

LEAVING CERTIFICATE EXAMINATION, 2017

English - Ordinary Level - Paper 1

Total Marks: 200

Wednesday, June 7th – Morning, 9.30 – 12.20

- This paper is divided into two sections,
  Section I COMPREHENDING and Section II COMPOSING.
- The paper contains **three** texts on the general theme of SCHOOL DAYS.
- Candidates should familiarise themselves with each of the texts before beginning their answers.

- Both sections of this paper (COMPREHENDING and COMPOSING) must be attempted.
- Each section carries 100 marks.

SECTION I - COMPREHENDING

- Two questions, A and B, follow each text.
- Candidates must answer a Question A on one text and a Question B on a different text. Candidates must answer only one Question A and only one Question B.
- **N.B.** Candidates may NOT answer a Question A and a Question B on the same text.

SECTION II - COMPOSING

- Candidates must write on **one** of the compositions 1 – 7.

Page 1 of 12 ➡

- **Read a different text and answer the Question B that follows it.** Question B also carries 50 marks, but it is usually a longer question inspired by the text. It can be a letter, magazine or newspaper article, talk or speech, blog, diary, report, advertisement, etc.

Question A (50 marks) + Question B (50 marks) = Total for Comprehending (100 marks)

Section 2 Composing (100 marks)

- The Composing section is sometimes called 'the essay question'.
- There are **seven options of compositions** and they are inspired by the three reading choices in Section 1.
- Compositions carry **100 marks**.
- Three or four options will be **narratives**, e.g. 'write a story'.
- Other options are **similar to Question B in Section 1** (e.g. write a speech, report or article) but are longer.

Total for Composing (100 marks)

Paper 2

Paper 2 has **three sections:**

Section 1 Single text option (60 marks)

- Your **teacher chooses a text** (novel or play) to be studied in detail.
- This is the text that you need to be most familiar with for the exam.
- You must answer **three short questions** on specific moments or issues in the story (10 marks + 10 marks + 10 marks = 30 marks).
- You must answer **one longer question** that requires analysis of bigger issues in the story. You will be given three longer questions to choose from and each will carry equal marks. Choose one to answer (30 marks).

Three short questions (30 marks) + one longer question (30 marks) = Total for Single Text Option (60 marks)

Section 2 Comparative study (70 marks)

- Your **teacher chooses two or three texts** (novels, plays or films).
- You **compare the texts** under specific headings or 'modes'.

MODES OF COMPARISON	
2018	**2019**
Social Setting	Theme
Relationships	Relationships
Hero, Heroine, Villain	Hero, Heroine, Villain

- **Three** such modes are **prescribed** for the exam each year.
- **Two of the three modes will appear on the paper.**
- **Choose one** of the two modes in the exam, **either A or B.**
- Each mode is usually broken into two parts: **Q1 or Q2. Choose one.**
- It is important to read all of these questions carefully and **make a good choice before you write anything.**
- **You will have two questions under the same mode on the texts you have studied.** The marks are usually divided into **30 marks + 40 marks** (70 marks).

Total for Comparative Study (70 marks)

Section 3 Poetry (70 marks)

A Unseen poem (20 marks)

- Usually a short and interesting poem that you read closely.
- Questions follow the poem. Sometimes there are two short questions of 10 marks each. Sometimes there is one longer question of 20 marks.

B Prescribed poetry (50 marks)

- There are 36 poems prescribed on the course.
- The poems are divided into two sections: 20 poems come from a combined Higher/Ordinary Level list and 16 poems come from a list of poems for Ordinary Level only.
- Teachers and students must be clear about which list of poems they will study closely. Revise one list or the other. There is no need to study 36 poems.
- Four poems will appear on the exam paper: two from one list and two from the other. Choose one poem on which to answer questions.
- Questions follow each poem. Typically they involve three short questions of 10 marks each, followed by one longer question of 20 marks.
- The question carrying 20 marks often asks you to be creative in your response, as opposed to simply explaining what the poem means.

A: Unseen Poem (20 marks) + B: Prescribed Poetry (50 marks) = Total for Poetry Section (70 marks)

Grand Total = 400 Marks

The day of the exam

Traditionally, the Leaving Certificate exam schedule has begun on the first Wednesday after the June bank holiday. You will be given English Paper 1 just before 9.30 a.m. that day. Thousands of students are given the opportunity to have their knowledge, understanding, skills and attitudes assessed and rewarded.

Nerves

- **Nervousness can be a powerfully positive force in pressure situations.**
  Most students will be nervous, but that is not a bad thing! Believe it or not, it is good to be nervous. By using this book, you will learn how to turn nerves into powerful and effective writing.

- **Your body and your brain are ready to perform!**
  Being **nervous** is physiological, which means it is something to do with your body's reaction to a pressure situation. Being **afraid** is different. It is a psychological state, which means that it is in your head. While both are interlinked, the physical signs of nervousness are an indication that you are physically prepared for the challenge.

Keep a positive attitude when revising. Try to enjoy the challenge of reading and writing.

You might experience sweaty palms as you hold your pen, increased heart rate as you await the paper and a funny feeling in your stomach. All of these signs are **normal and healthy**. Remember that anybody who ever achieved anything of great merit felt exactly the same way. Most students in the exam hall will feel this way, too. So don't get upset by being nervous. It is the way most people will feel.

The three Cs

Clarity

Clarity means being **clear**. It is absolutely essential that you are clear about what the English exam entails and also what each individual question asks of you. Each chapter in this book will begin with a set of **aims**. Examine the aims closely, so that you **know what you are trying to achieve**. Throughout the book, typical questions for each section will be outlined. Sample answers will be provided, along with close detail on how such answers are graded. A timing guide will also be given and key points will be emphasised. All of these elements will ensure that you have clarity.

To write well, you need: **CLARITY, COHERENCE** and **CONFIDENCE**. These elements are reflected in the marking scheme.

Coherence

Coherence means **making sense**. Having worked out what each exam question means, the aim is to write coherent answers. Many teachers and examiners will tell you that students frequently fail to **answer the**

question asked. Others fail to answer the right number of questions or simply do not **make sensible choices in the exam** itself. If you have worries about spelling and grammar, try to focus on answering the right questions and making sense. You will be rewarded.

Confidence

Every student wants to be confident. It is actually nothing more than **your feelings about yourself. In order to increase your confidence, you must keep reading and practising your writing.** Then what you write, and how you write it, will be greatly improved. Examiners look for answers that show a broad command of English as well as a student's individual way of responding. If you work hard and feel confident, your efforts will pay off.

Having a **positive attitude** is the starting point for getting good grades in your exams.

2017. M.10

**Coimisiún na Scrúduithe Stáit
State Examinations Commission**

LEAVING CERTIFICATE EXAMINATION, 2017

English - Ordinary Level - Paper 2

Total Marks: 200

Thursday, 8th June – Afternoon, 2.00 – 5.20

Candidates must attempt the following:

- **ONE** question from SECTION I – The Single Text
- **ONE** question from SECTION II – The Comparative Study
- **THE QUESTIONS** on the Unseen Poem from SECTION III – Poetry
- The questions on **ONE** of the Prescribed Poems from SECTION III – Poetry

INDEX OF SINGLE TEXTS	
Emma	- Page 2
Circle of Friends	- Page 3
The Great Gatsby	- Page 4
A Doll's House	- Page 5
Big Maggie	- Page 6
Death and Nightingales	- Page 7
The Plough and the Stars	- Page 8
The Spinning Heart	- Page 9
Hamlet	- Page 10

Page 1 of 20 ➡

2 The Marking Scheme

- To understand exactly how the exam is marked, through detailed analysis of two comprehension answers.
- To show the link between **content** (what you write) and **style** (how you write).

How the exam is marked

Examiners do not mark your work according to their opinion or guesswork. Every answer is marked according to specific headings outlined below.

Always aim to write as much as you can in the time allowed, once it is relevant to the question.

Note

Examiners' Assessments appear throughout the book. You will notice that these contain a breakdown of marks awarded. Marking is done by reference to the **PCLM** criteria for assessment:

- Clarity of purpose (P): 30% of the total.
- Coherence of delivery (C): 30% of the total.
- Efficiency of language use (L): 30% of the total.
- Accuracy of mechanics (M): 10% of the total.

Clarity of purpose (30%)

This is explained as 'engagement with the set task', which is a fancy way of asking whether or not you have **answered the question that was asked**. It also means that you must have a **personal, original answer**. You will be rewarded for honesty and for sticking to what the question asks of you. For example, when you are asked if you **like or dislike the Unseen Poem**, the first sentence of your answer should immediately state **whether you like or dislike it**. This should be followed by your reasons and backed up with quotations and support.

Coherence of delivery (30%)

This aspect concerns structure. Have you **constructed your answer in a logical fashion** with statement, quotation and comment? Do you **make sense** from beginning to end? You are expected to deal with one point per paragraph and to have your ideas ordered in a logical sequence. For example, essays should have a clear beginning, middle and end.

Efficiency of language use (30%)

This refers to your vocabulary, your fluency with words and your phrasing of ideas. In simple terms, it is **how** you write, as opposed to **what** you write. You can never have enough practice in this area. Language skills often determine your final grade.

Accuracy of mechanics (10%)

This refers to spelling and grammar, as well as the correct placement of words in sentences. While you won't be penalised for every error, **poor mechanics can have a negative effect on your overall grade.**

	SIMPLE GUIDE	
1.	Answer the question asked	(30%)
2.	Make sense in your answer	(30%)
3.	Use good vocabulary and expressions	(30%)
4.	Spell correctly	(10%)

NB! – the marking scheme tells examiners that the individual marks for C, L and M cannot be greater than P. What does this mean for students?

Answering the question asked is the most important thing to do in the exam. Focus very closely on what exactly the questions ask you to do.

The most common mistakes made by candidates are:

- writing responses that don't answer the question

OR

- not choosing the correct questions

This is what causes students to lose the most marks every year.

key point

The **content** of your answer (**what** you write) covers 60% of the total marks in every question. The **style** (**how** you write) counts for 40%.

Observe how each Sample Answer is marked according to PCLM throughout the book and try to make your own answers more exam-focused!

Sample Questions and Sample Marking

Below is a reproduction of the first comprehension question from the **2016 Ordinary Level Exam.**

- What follows is a **15-mark question** from **Part A** with a student's answer.
- Then, there is a **50-mark question** from **Part B** with a different student's response.
- Read the passage and look closely at **how these answers were marked.**
- Before reading the examiner's assessment, **try to work out the mark that you think the student deserves.** See if you are close to the actual mark.

Section One – Comprehension (LC 2016, OL)

Text 3 – Keeping a Diary

This text is an edited adaptation of an article by Michael Palin from *The Guardian* newspaper. Michael Palin is famous as a member of the Monty Python comedy group and for his TV travel documentaries. Here he writes about his experience of keeping a diary for almost fifty years, and offers advice to would-be diary keepers.

1. When I began to keep a diary in April 1969, I could scarcely have imagined that decades of my life would not only be recorded but later published for all to see. I was twenty-five years old when I took a crisp new ring-backed notepad, headed the page '1969', and wrote more in hope than in expectation.

2. I have always been attracted to lists, and the ultimate for any list keeper is to keep a record of what you've done each day; a diary, in fact. All I'd lacked in the past was the will to keep at it. Very little happened on that first day of the new diary, or so it seemed at the time. Yet when I reread my diary entry for Thursday, April 17th, 1969, my diary reminds me that I had David Jason [Del Boy in *Only Fools and Horses*] around for lunch, and took a phone call about a possible new show with John Cleese [Basil in *Fawlty Towers*, Monty Python member]. If I had not kept a diary I would never remember all this.

3. That's the attraction of a diary. It remains in its own time. It reflects only what happened on that particular day. It doesn't flatter and it isn't influenced by what happened later. In that way it's the most truthful record of real life, and that's why I'm so glad I persevered with it.

4. There are times when I've had to drive myself to do it. Times when I had so little time to write that I just jotted down a few notes, but mostly I've tried to approach each morning's entry as a story of the day that has just passed, without limits and without self-censorship. And composing a story a day is not a bad discipline for any would-be writer.

5. I never wrote with the idea of publication in mind. I don't think I even wrote for another reader. Occasionally I would read a piece to my wife, usually to settle an argument about what we had or hadn't done. But the longer I kept the diaries the more I saw them gathering some sort of historical relevance. Something that happened the day before might have little significance at the time, but twenty-five or thirty years later it acquires an extra dimension.

6. Thanks to the diaries I can remember things that I would almost certainly have forgotten. For a diarist, life ceases to be an indistinct blur. Experiences are there in sharp focus; some an immeasurable pleasure, others a profound pain, which is the way life is. This is why diary-keeping is often prescribed as a therapy for those with depression, or those who feel their lives are somehow out of control. I encourage you to do as I did all those years ago; get your own notebook out and write down the year and the day and what happened to you in the last twenty-four hours. And keep on doing it. I try and get down what I can remember in thirty minutes maximum.

7. I've found the diary habit very helpful to my own development as a writer. You have to be able to think clearly and edit as you go. An online blog is fine, but I feel very strongly that it's not the same thing as writing down your own experiences in your own hand, in your own chosen notebook. Handwriting is so much more personal. It expresses your personality. I can tell from mine how I was feeling at the time – sometimes hurried and rushed, sometimes relaxed and expansive.

8. You may find it hard, as I did, to find time to write. You may get discouraged by days when nothing seems to happen. Don't give up. I found that details of what you ate or who you were with or what music you were listening to might seem insignificant at the time, but as the years go by these are the things you, and others, really want to know about. Tastes and circumstances change so fast that it is often hardly believable that this is what we did then, this is how we lived, and this is what we were all worried about. The diarist keeps tabs on us all.

9. Keeping a diary means that all that seeing and hearing, loving and laughing, excitement and embarrassment, gladness and gloom that go to make up a life are not forgotten. In short, a diary blows away the mists of time, and offers your life back to you.

Question A (i)

What do you learn about Michael Palin from reading the above text? Support your answer with reference to the text.

(15 marks)

SAMPLE ANSWER

> I think Michael Palin is a thoughtful person who likes to keep things organised. He is thoughtful because he says that a diary is 'the most truthful record of real life.' He has been keeping records of his daily adventures since 1969 so he obviously enjoys thinking back over each day and then remembering how things went for him many

years later. He is organised, simply because keeping a diary that long takes effort. He says that 'you have to be able to think clearly and edit as you go along.' He sounds like a man who likes things to be clear and simple to follow. That's why he writes a diary that is easy to read afterwards.

(117 words)

NOTES ON THE MARKING SCHEME

- For 15-mark questions, the first two headings (purpose and coherence) are combined, as are the other two (language and mechanics)
- This happens for all questions which have <u>less than 30 marks</u>
- The 15 marks are then divided as follows:
  9 marks for WHAT is written
  6 marks for HOW it is written

EXAMINER'S ASSESSMENT

The student does answer the question asked and provides two quotations with following explanations. At 117 words, including two points with quotation and explanation, this is precisely what a 15-mark answer should read like. The vocabulary provided is of a very good standard and there are no errors in 'mechanics' i.e. spelling and grammar.

MARKS AWARDED

P+C	=	9
L+M	=	6
Total	=	15 /15 (O1 Grade)

key point

Effort is rewarded at ordinary level. Answer the question asked, as best you can, in the time allowed.

Now look at **Question B**, which follows.

- You cannot choose the B question from the same text as the A question. A **different student's response is found here.**

exam focus

Students can't choose the B question from the same text as the A question.

- In this case, the four aspects of marking – purpose, coherence, language and mechanics – are divided separately to give a breakdown of **15+15+15+5 = 50 marks.**
- This is the case for all questions which have **30 marks or more.**

Question B

Write an article, to appear either in your school magazine or on your school's website, in which you offer advice to your fellow students on finding a part-time job for the summer holidays. Your advice should include tips about where to find work, how to make a successful application and how to prepare for an interview.

(50 marks)

SAMPLE ANSWER

Hi everyone. Stacy here once again with my monthly update on all things trending and happening in the world of St Mary's. As this is the final instalment before the exams next month, I think it's a good time to put aside all thoughts of June and instead think about the glorious summer of freedom ahead.

There is one major problem however, all that celebrating and partying is going to cost you a pretty penny. And given that most of us are gone beyond pestering our parents for money, now is the time to seriously consider seeking out some part time work. Getting a job isn't as simple as you might think. And employers expect certain things from you in return. So here are my five key tips to securing a job for the summer.

1) Apply for a variety of jobs. Don't decide beforehand that your only going to work in a pub or an office. It doesn't happen that way. Start with the obvious things like bar or restaurant work, shop assistant, working with a small local business or handing out leaflets for charity. Once you keep applying, something will eventually come your way.

2) Be willing to work hard for little money. This might not sound great but it is the reality. We all have to start at the bottom. Just deal with it. If you want money, then this will mean making sacrifices.

3) Be polite and friendly, but not too much, when speaking to a potential employer. Nobody will employ somebody who gives off a nasty or grumpy air when you meet them. You are young, skilled and enthusiastic so don't be afraid to let that shine in an interview or job application.

4) Always be on time, most especially if you have an interview for a job. If you cannot be on time for an interview it is very likely that you will not be employed as a result. If you get a reputation for being late, taking too many breaks or coming in with a hangover, then you won't last long.

5) Think about how you should dress yourself for the job. Work is not usually an excuse to get dressed up and flaunt yourself, unless you fancy being a part-time model. Working with a horse trainer, for example, might involve a lot of long hours and muck and dirt. If going to the races, then you will be expected to look professional and stylish. But remember that it is the horse, not you, that is the centre of attention. Also, if it is a job that has a specific uniform, like in a restaurant, then bear in mind what this will look like to the customers. You must always try to look professional and tidy.

There are many other things to think about but if you keep these five in mind, you should definitely get work of some kind this summer.

Until next year!

Stacy

(494 words)

EXAMINER'S ASSESSMENT

This is an **excellent** effort. At 494 words, it is **long enough**, addressing the question as required. The **register (language, tone, purpose)** is **appropriate to a school magazine**. This deserves good marks. It is **well-structured**: five different pieces of advice are offered, which is a good way to answer the 50 mark task. **Vocabulary** is of an excellent standard. There are very few **spelling/grammar** errors to note.

MARKS AWARDED

15 + 15 + 15 + 5 = 50/50 (O1 Grade)

Further details of how the English Exam is marked can be found at **www.examinations.ie**. Follow the links to the relevant papers.

3 Language Genres in the Exam

In studying Leaving Certificate Ordinary Level English, you need to be familiar with five genres:

1. **Informative language:** the language of information.
2. **Narrative language:** the language of story.
3. **Persuasive language:** the language of persuasion.
4. **Argumentative language:** the language of logic.
5. **Aesthetic language:** the language of beauty and style.

- **Informative language** is all around you. It is **direct**, **factual**, **objective** and should be **easy to understand**. You will employ lots of informative language in your exam answers.

- **Narrative language** is found in **stories**, **diaries** and **personal essays**. Not all students who like to tell stories are necessarily good at writing them. (Chapter 5 will help you to make this decision for yourself.)

- **Persuasive language** attempts to put forward a point of view or opinion in a way that might **influence** other people. It is often **emotive**. This means that it touches people's **feelings** more than their logic or sense. It is used in political speeches and is essential in good advertising and various other strands of the media. It is likely that you will use persuasive language in many of your answers.

- **Argumentative language** is the language of logic and argument. It is less concerned with emotive language than with **logical**, **rational** thought and speech. A **debate** is by definition an argument. While argument tries to remain cold and **factual**, persuasion contains more emotion and suggestion. You may find questions in Paper 2 that ask you to argue for or against a viewpoint. The wording of these questions often contains the phrase: 'Do you agree with ...?'

- **Aesthetic language** is found in works of **literature**, such as poetry, drama and cinema. It is considered **beautiful** or **stylish** language and can be called 'aesthetically pleasing'. This quality gives writing its colour, humour, power and vitality.

These five language genres are all around you every day. The more you read and the more you look, the more you will recognise them.

Recognising the genres

What follows are **five short passages**, all of which refer to the same concept: a cake. In each case, identify which of the genres is being used.

> 1. Cakes are an essential feature of most modern wedding celebrations. I would argue that to replace such a standard cake with a jelly and ice-cream monstrosity is illogical and foolish. I also fear that it will cause an unwanted mess due to its likely melting before the main course is finished.

> 2. Take the cake mixture, already well settled, and place in a non-stick baking dish. Smooth around the edges and ensure that none of the mixture contains lumps. Cover with a baking sheet and place in a preheated oven at 180 degrees centigrade. Cook for two hours, or until the top is golden and crispy. Allow to settle before removing from the dish.

> 3. The scoop of the spoon, the bend of the bowl. The sweep of mother's hand as she gathers the precious remaining grains of flavour into her cloudy, floury fingers. With a final few stirs and whips, the gluey mixture is ready for its final journey to the cavernous oven. Then the real moment of tension: the split second before mother tosses the utensils to the waiting sink. It is all the time he needs. With an innocent, pleading grin, he gently swipes the sugar-and-dough coated delicacy. Wooden spoons never tasted so good.

4. The day Henry decided to bake his own wedding cake was the day it started to go wrong. While it might seem inappropriate now to blame divorce on such trivial matters, wars have been fought over less. Anyway, Henry was a stubborn type, insisting on an ice-cream monstrosity despite advice from those who knew better.

5. As one who speaks for the marginalised of this society, I implore you all to donate any unwanted cakes for the upcoming charity cake sale. Your company produces more than five hundred cakes a week, some of which end up being thrown out because of a lack of demand from your regular customers. Can you really continue with this thoughtless policy, as others beg for scraps of food to survive? You have the power to bring about change.

Did you notice the specific features of each genre?

1. **Argumentative** language appeals to logic and sense, e.g. a jelly and ice-cream cake is likely to melt.
2. **Informative** language is mostly factual. In this case, we read the instructions for successfully baking a cake.
3. **Aesthetic** language rises above the ordinary and the purely informative. This beautiful and colourful description of a childhood memory stimulates our imagination.
4. **Narrative** language tells a story, as in the story of poor Henry whose stubbornness gets him into trouble.
5. **Persuasive** language tugs at your feelings, e.g. pleading with the reader to consider the needy in society.

> exam focus
>
> If you are familiar with different language genres, you will find it easier to answer questions.

Your teacher has probably helped you become familiar with examples of each genre. In many cases, a piece of writing will contain **combinations** of the above. For practice, re-read Chapter 1 and find examples of each genre.

 **Comprehension**

- To examine the **types of questions** that occur in the Comprehension section.
- To understand the importance of **choosing the questions wisely** before answering any of them.

While the Comprehension section appears straightforward, it does amount to **25 per cent of your final total**, so treat it with care.

Comprehension means to understand something. The Comprehension section is a fairly gentle start to your Leaving Certificate, since the questions aim to test your ability to respond logically and creatively to questions on a given text.

Three or four different **extracts** will appear on the exam paper. These will consist of written pieces usually from a magazine, book, newspaper or other source.

There are two types of questions to answer:

- **Question A:** broken into three parts and amounting to 50 marks in total.
- **Question B:** a single question requiring a longer answer and also amounting to 50 marks in total.

You must choose one Question A for one text and one Question B for a different text.

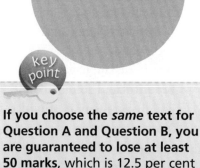

25%

key point

If you choose the *same* text for Question A and Question B, you are guaranteed to lose at least 50 marks, which is 12.5 per cent of the total. This can mean a serious drop in your final grade. Do not make this mistake!

How to approach the Comprehension section

Take time to **read all of the comprehensions. Choose your Question B first.** This is a more demanding exercise, so you should pick the one you feel best suits you. Then select your **Question A.** The standard is similar across all questions. **Once your choice is made, answer Question A and then Question B.** The most important rule for Comprehension questions is: **answer the question asked.**

Language genres in the Comprehension section

Informative language

All of the texts contain information. This is factual, impersonal language. It is not emotive and it speaks directly, e.g. *Hamlet was the Prince of Denmark.* **It is most likely that A questions will ask you to locate specific pieces of information in the given text.**

> **Choose your questions carefully!** Choose Question B, then choose Question A. Once you've made your choice, complete Question A first, then Question B.

Narrative language

This language tells a story. Clearly you need information to tell a story, so there will be some crossover with informative language here. But narration happens in a time and place (setting) and uses words to create situations, images, feelings and reactions. For example: *I will always remember the day that I broke my leg.* **Narration is likely to be found in B questions.**

Persuasive language

Persuasion involves one-sided opinion, often with emotion attached. You might remember your Junior Certificate Media Studies section. It highlighted the role of persuasive language in advertising, along with buzzwords and slogans, e.g. *8 out of 10 cats prefer it; Unbeatable value at our new store; The time for change has come, etc.* **B questions that involve a talk with an audience, advertisement scripts or political speeches must all involve persuasive language.**

Argumentative language

An argument presents facts in a clear, logical and convincing way. For example: *Uniforms should be compulsory in schools for the following three reasons...* Each of your A answers should read like a short argument, where you tackle the question by using evidence selected from the text. **Most comprehension exercises involve arguing your point in a logical and clear way.** B questions, such as a debate or journalistic article, are likely to involve argument.

Aesthetic language

All good writing is aesthetically pleasing, even if you don't immediately recognise this quality. But what is aesthetic language? A simple way of understanding this is to ask: **does it sound good to read?** This happens when we write answers as if we were artists enjoying our work, rather than students struggling to succeed.

> 'Students struggling to succeed' is a simple example of alliteration, an aesthetic feature. 'The exam is a marathon' is a metaphor. 'The exam hall is like a pressure cooker' is a simile. All of these features of language show how we can elevate and improve our expression through the use of aesthetics. You can write like this too!

Comprehension: 'A' Questions (50 marks/ 35 minutes)

- These short questions will ask you:
  - **What** is the writer saying?
  - **How** does the writer say it?
  - What is your **response** to it?
- Each question will be marked out of **10, 15 or 20 marks. All the questions in the section will add up to a total of 50 marks.**
- You must **write a little more** and think carefully about any 20-mark questions.
- It is a good idea to read the questions first, **underlining key words** so as to work out the **purpose** of the question.
- This allows your mind to figure out answers **subconsciously** as you read.

Sample Question – 2015 Exam Paper, Text 2

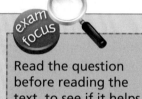

'THE REAL MRS BROWN'

This adapted text is based on edited extracts from **The Real Mrs Brown: Brendan O'Carroll,** *an authorised biography by Brian Beacom. In it we discover the influence of Brendan O'Carroll's mother, Maureen, on his popular sitcom character, Agnes Brown.*

Read the question before reading the text, to see if it helps you form an answer.

1. Flashback to 17 September, 1911 in Dublin City, Ireland. Seventeen-year-old Lizzie was set to marry Michael McHugh. The pair were madly in love and ready to head to America together to start a new life – but without telling Lizzie's parents. Lizzie's father was deeply against them marrying. When he heard of their romance he attacked Michael, breaking his forearm and collarbone. Michael and Lizzie knew that they had to escape Ireland. That's why they had saved for a year to buy tickets for the long sea voyage. But Lizzie's mother found out about the plan and convinced her husband he had to accept Michael, or he'd lose his daughter forever. Michael and Lizzie's father shook hands and the next day Michael McHugh put an advertisement in the newspaper offering his boat tickets for sale. The ship they would have sailed on was the *Titanic*.

2. Meanwhile, Lizzie and Michael became Mr and Mrs McHugh and a child was born: a baby girl. She was christened Maureen and she was to become Brendan O'Carroll's mother, the woman who provided most of the inspiration for Brendan's sitcom heroine, Agnes Brown. Speaking of his mother, Brendan O'Carroll said, 'People used to ask me if Agnes Brown was based on my mother and I'd say no. But in recent times, I've come to realise just how close they are.'

Indeed. Both are battlers. Both could find a colourful adjective when roused, although Maureen was smarter and way more ambitious than the havoc-creating, uneducated, Agnes Brown. Maureen could definitely deliver a cutting one-liner, just as Agnes does. Maureen could also take a simple tea towel and turn it into a weapon, as Agnes frequently does. Both Maureen and Agnes would lay down their lives for their kids, but loved to make fun of them. Brendan's mammy also had the ability to get what she wanted out of people, just as Agnes can, using the cleverest of psychology, becoming a bit pathetic when required. And if that didn't work, like Agnes, she would tell the world exactly where it was going wrong.

3. Maureen's healthy disrespect for authority – life is to be challenged and rules are there to be broken – is evident in Agnes. As Agnes does, Maureen lived in crowded houses, and managed to create her own safe little world. There are more similarities. Maureen wasn't entirely comfortable with modern devices either. She had little time for small-minded people. Agnes Brown now and Maureen O'Carroll then would be ready and willing to smack the face of injustice.

4. Maureen had incredible energy and studied hard, and her reward was to be sent to University College Galway, a rare achievement for a woman at that time. She

became a teacher of languages, and loved her career. But on the day she married Gerry O'Carroll in 1936, she was fired from her job as it was illegal for female teachers in Ireland to be married. Did Maureen O'Carroll take this lying down? 'My mother was a force of nature,' Brendan recalls. 'She said, "I'm not having that!" and joined the union and battled to get that law changed. She shares that feisty, fighting spirit with Agnes Brown.'

5. It wasn't a huge surprise when the Irish Labour Party asked her to run for parliament, Dáil Éireann. But it was a surprise when she won in the General Election of 1954. It was remarkable for a working-class female to achieve that level of success. What made it all the more extraordinary was that she had given birth to nine children. And, in what offers an insight into the character of Maureen O'Carroll, one of her kids, Phil, was adopted.

6. Why does Mrs Brown's Boys work? It's Agnes Brown, of course. Every family has one: the busybody, the scathing commentator, the woman with a sharp tongue who can still hug her kids like they are babies.

Question (i)

Based on Maureen O'Carroll's experiences, outlined in the extract above, which word or words from the following do you think best describe the situation experienced by many women in Ireland in the past?

Challenging   Difficult   Unequal

Explain your answer, supporting the points you make by reference to the text.

(15 marks)

SAMPLE ANSWER

I think the words 'challenging' and 'unequal' are two words that describe the situation for women in Ireland in the past. It seems that women were expected to get married and have many children back in the time of Maureen O'Carroll. There was a great challenge in feeding and clothing so many children. She had nine, which is very unusual for today. It is very unequal because she had to quit her job as a teacher. To me that sounds very wrong. It was wrong then and is wrong today still.

EXAMINER'S ASSESSMENT

The candidate chooses two words, but does not adequately expand upon each of them. This answer would be better if the candidate made a **POINT**, by choosing one word and then using a **QUOTATION** to support the choice. It would benefit from have some follow-up **EXPLANATION** or commentary after that. For the full 15 marks, **TWO brief points**, well made, is usually sufficient. This answer is perhaps too brief and lacking development to score highly. The candidate does show some level of **understanding**, however, and the answer is broadly correct. Language and mechanics are **basic but correct**.

MARKS AWARDED

5 + 4 = 9/15 (O4 Grade)

> **key point**
>
> Answers require you to follow the 'POINT-QUOTE-EXPLAIN' formula for each paragraph you write.

Comprehension: 'B' Questions (50 marks/35 minutes)

B questions could be considered 'short essay' questions. These questions test your personal writing skills within a closely defined task. Therefore you must always bear in mind **what the task is.**

> **key point**
>
> Remember this as a golfer would: you are trying to score a **par** on each question. Always know your purpose, audience and register for each question on Paper 1.

Each B question will have:

- A specific **purpose**: what you must write.
- A stated **audience**: to whom the piece is addressed.
- A particular **register**: the piece must sound right.

PURPOSE, AUDIENCE, REGISTER

The **purpose** and the **audience** will be indicated in the question itself. Close reading of the questions will reveal them to you.

However, **register** is more difficult to define. The scenarios below will help you to understand and find the right register:

- Imagine speaking to a small child and explaining something complicated. You will use certain words and phrases and take a gentle tone in order to be understood. You would not speak the same way to an adult about the same issue. You expect that the adult will understand differently, so you change your language and tone to suit the audience.

- Explaining the economic situation to a group of students in university will require lots of factual analysis and statistical data. A politician explaining the economic situation to voters will need a much more careful (and perhaps emotive) approach in order to be understood.

key point

Register is a blend of suitable **vocabulary**, **tone** and **treatment of the task**.

Types of B Questions

By looking at past papers, you will notice that some B questions require similar answers. They can be grouped into types in order to help with revision and practice.

1. Writing for media

Examples include:

- **Review**
- **Newspaper article**
- **Report**
- **Commentary on an event**
- **Advertisement script**
- **Blog.**

This type of question involves writing for the media. Questions can take many forms, but there are overall similarities within the type.

If you like to read newspapers, blog or follow current affairs, a media-type question may suit you. Perhaps there is a journalist or sports commentator inside you waiting to get out! If you like **expressing opinions to a broad audience**, consider this option on the exam paper.

In questions that involve writing for media, there is bound to be lots of opinion. Sometimes **bias** can occur when a writer takes a very one-sided view of a situation. Since this is a creative exercise, a one-sided view could make for very good reading, e.g. a sports commentator with a very strong preference for one team over another can write very entertaining pieces.

SAMPLE QUESTION – MEDIA ARTICLE 2014 EXAM

Note: this type of question – **writing for or speaking to your peers or some group of students** – has become a regular type of question in recent years. The 'purpose–audience–register' guide for this is very useful.

Question

Write an article for your school magazine about two or more interesting people you would like to meet and explain why you would like to meet them.

(50 marks)

SAMPLE ANSWER:

My name is Shane. I'm a typical Irish 17-year-old. Most lads my age have little or no interest in politics. So you might find it a bit unusual, readers, for me to say that I would like to meet with two fairly famous politicians, one Irish and one American. If I had a choice, I would like to have a cup of tea with Michael D. Higgins and Donald Trump at the same time.

I say tea because I am too young to drink – well I'm supposedly too young – but you get what I mean. I would be afraid what would happen if the three of us, especially the 'Don', got a few too many tipples and starting arguing about something controversial. Like, for instance, Galway United Football Club, a thing that Michael D. is passionate about. I'd say Mr Trump would know very little about Galway. Or anything united come to think of it.

But anyway, my main interest in meeting these two powerful men is to see what exactly motivates them. Why did they choose to get into an area where you get abuse and criticism every day and a lot of the time people poke fun at you? Why would anybody like that?

Yes, there is a lot of money and fame to come from being a president, not to mention the pride you might feel. But I would want to know if it is really worth it as a lot of politicians seem to get old and fat once they get into the job.

There is another question I would ask the two of them. It is to do with relationships. I think it is a little bit unfair – I must be careful with the word little – but our president gets slagged and teased because he is so small. Does it matter to him? People get bullied in school for all kinds of things and being small, weak or timid is one of them.

It is the opposite with Mr Trump. He is big, loud and aggressive. He comes across as the bully a lot of the time, complaining about immigrants, Mexicans, women or whoever was annoying him on Twitter the previous night. So my main idea would be to get the two of these men into a room and see if the bully boy can get the better of the little guy in the corner. Now that would be a great meeting to be at.

Something tells me my money would be on Michael D. He has seen so much in life, having to look up to so many people. He now looks down proudly but respectfully at his Irish nation. He could teach Mr Trump a few things about that. This is why I would love to have a cup of tea with Michael D. and Mr Trump. It would be worth the price of the biscuits!

(485 words)

EXAMINER'S ASSESSMENT

This is wonderfully **engaging, creative answer**. It addresses the specific task with a **witty and entertaining register**. It is broken into **distinct and coherent paragraphs** to indicate clear progression of ideas, each one linked. The **vocabulary** is easy to read, **uncomplicated but precise**. The meaning is very clear throughout. Mechanics are **very good**. This is an example of a candidate who runs with **a simple idea** and expresses some **imaginative thoughts** in a clear way. It is a **high-scoring effort**.

MARKS AWARDED

15 + 15 + 15 + 5 = 50/50 (O1 Grade)

2. Letters and diary entries

These answers must be written with the assumption that very few people, if any, will get to read them. They are often much more **personal** and **intimate** than other forms. Sometimes they can be **formal**, as in a formal or business letter.

If you feel comfortable **expressing your feelings** in a diary, or if you write letters when the opportunity arises, you should consider this type of question. Some people find it **easier to write things down** rather than say them directly to another person. If you are like this, letters and diary entries might be suitable forms for you.

Revise the section on **diary entries** in Chapter 2. Study the example, sample answer and marking scheme there. Below you will find more information on **letters**.

SAMPLE QUESTION – LETTER 2015 EXAM

Question
You have decided to apply for a weekend job in a pet shop, Wacker's in Donaghmede, Dublin. Write the letter of application you would submit to the Manager of the pet shop.

(50 marks)

SAMPLE ANSWER:

> 23 Ramblers Lane
> Swords Road
> Co Dublin
> 19th May 2018

Dear Sir/Madam

My name is Harry Macken and I am 16 years old. I read the advertisement for the job in your store 'Wacker's Pet Shop' in Donaghmede. I would like to apply for this job for the upcoming summer break.

I have some experience working with animals. My uncle Sean has a collection of racing pigeons. I have worked with him for six years in looking after the pigeons and would consider myself quite skilled in dealing with all kinds of birds. I see that you have a large collection of finches, budgies and parakeets in your shop so my experience in this field would be valuable.

We have also had family pets such as dogs, cats and goldfish over the previous years. My mother put me in charge of our pet greyhound when I was 12. Unfortunately, he was run over by a van. Because of this, I am aware of how people can get very close to their pets. I know how upset people get when their pet gets injured or dies. I think this would be very valuable to you in helping people choose the right pet for them.

I am hard-working, well-behaved and willing to work long hours for the money. I get on well with people and I get on even better with animals. I have a kind personality.

I enclose a C.V. which I did in my transition year class in school. The name of my references are at the bottom. I look forward to working with you if you could offer me this job.

Yours sincerely,

Harry Macken

(267 words)

EXAMINER'S ASSESSMENT

The candidate does write a letter and it is set out in the **format and style of one**. The **expression is basic** and to the point while the **vocabulary is adequate**. The answer is quite brief for 50 marks and would benefit from greater emphasis on why the applicant wants the job. Overall, a solid answer, just short of high marks.

MARKS AWARDED

12 + 11 + 11 + 4 = 38/50 (O3 Grade)

3. Speeches and talks

These questions are for you if you can imagine yourself before an audience delivering a powerful speech or informative talk. If you have watched great **public speakers** such as politicians and leaders delivering speeches, copy their approach in your writing. Remember a time when you saw your school principal or another teacher give an **informative talk**. Perhaps you have experienced great team-talks given by **sports coaches** or mentors. Can you do the same in your writing?

In these answers, you are aiming to be both **informative** and **emotive**: you want people to understand you, but you also want them to **feel a certain way**.

SAMPLE QUESTION – SPEECH 2012 EXAM

Question
Imagine you are running for election as leader of the Student Council in your school. Write the talk you would deliver to your school assembly outlining the qualities you feel you possess that would make you an excellent leader of the Student Council.

(50 marks)

SAMPLE ANSWER:

Mr Murphy, Fr Breen, my fellow classmates, teachers, ladies and gentlemen,

I Stephen Frank, your most esteemed classmate and friend, would like you to support my bid to become leader of our student council. This group of people has been central to so many of the improvements in the lives of the student population over the past ten years. Before we had a council, the students had no proper voice on which to speak their minds. That time is past and now it is time for a new leader to step up to the plate and drive this community forward.

I am a man to be rekoned with. I don't let people put me down or allow our rights to be taken from us. In first year, I was part of the student protest over the state of the canteen and the fact that food was not being cooked properly. This led to protests and I was right on the front line then. I will be on the front line once again in leading this student body in speaking our minds over important issues that effect us every day of every week.

I have shown my leadership skills before. I was part of the Under 16 hurling team that got to the munster playoffs two years ago. Again I was to the front in driving home this team to victory, even if we came up short in the final hurdle. I am hungry for success and there won't be a game of two halves with me. We will take victory in the first half and succeed from there.

I am a good listener and if any student has a problem in class I will be there to listen to you. I will not allow students rights to be walked on and I am the man to sort out any trouble. Just call by the third floor area any day and you will meet me there and I can then take all your issues forward to the school principle.

So everybody, listen up to me and take my advice: vote me Stephen Frank, the man who won't let you down.

(358 words)

EXAMINER'S ASSESSMENT

The candidate does make a fair attempt at writing a talk to be delivered at a school assembly. However, this answer contains a lot of cliché and empty rhetoric – it is unlikely that this type of language would prove convincing in a talk. The purpose is easily understood but it is a poorly phrased answer in many places, and there are a number of spelling and grammar errors. Vocabulary is quite limited; the speech lacks sincerity and sentences sound awkward – 'short in the final hurdle' and 'vote me Stephen Frank' are such examples.

MARKS AWARDED

8 + 7 + 7 + 3 = 25/50 (O5 Grade)

4. Visual texts

Some students are more comfortable answering a question that is based upon a picture or a set of 'visuals' that appear on the exam paper. When analysing a visual, some basic points must be kept in mind.

Context

The well-known 'w' questions apply here: **where**, **when**, **who**, **why** and **what**. They give us a sense of what the picture is about. Try to guess the context when you first look at the visual.

Purpose

Context will go some way towards understanding the **purpose** of the visual. The picture has been taken for a reason. Guess what that reason might be.

Point of view

From what angle do we see the picture? Is it close-up, long-distance, high-angle, low-angle, hidden, panoramic (seeing everything at once), etc?

Framing

What is in the picture frame? Certain details are included and certain details are left out. Consider elements such as: background, foreground, left, right, centre, corners, middle, positioning, etc.

Colour

Colour affects the way you feel about a picture.

- Bright colours such as yellows and oranges suggest happiness. Red can signify power, danger and adventure.

- Blue is the universal colour for calm. However, it can also suggest unhappiness ('the blues').
- Green is usually the colour for health and the environment. It is especially connected to Ireland and Irishness.
- Black and white visuals can suggest a particular atmosphere or capture a particular time. Remember context here: try to work out why the picture is in colour or black and white.
- Black and white visuals ask you to look more carefully at specific elements like shape and texture. They are also excellent for portraying facial expressions or capturing an event from the past.

The comprehension questions that accompany visual texts will ask you to **interpret or respond to what you see in the picture.**

You could follow the **statement–quotation–comment** approach that many teachers encourage in their classes:

key point

When responding to visual texts, **imagine being in the picture**.

- **State** what you see.
- **Quote** by mentioning specific details in the picture.
- **Comment** by backing up your view.

In recent exam papers, students have been asked to pay close attention to the 'visuals' that are found with the comprehensions. It is unknown whether you will be asked a question worth 10, 15 even 50 marks. However, a question of some sort is quite likely. Here is a sample question and answer based upon a visual from the 2014 exam. It is worth 50 marks. Remember the time allowed here is about 35 minutes. The response is in the form of a letter.

exam Q

SAMPLE QUESTION – VISUAL COMPREHENSION QUESTION 2013 EXAM

Question

Look at IMAGE 2. Write a letter to Roy Keane outlining what you like or dislike about him based upon this image. Say what you learn about him from looking at this image.

(50 marks)

SAMPLE ANSWER:

Dear Roy,

Firstly, my name is James. I have little or no interest in football but I have been a fan of yours for a number of years. This might seem strange since you are mostly famous as a football legend. But my main interest in your work stems from the fact that my brother Fergal is blind. He is now 14 years old but he still depends heavily upon the family for his daily needs. Most of all though, he has the most wonderful, kind and loyal guide dog named Jacko, who looks just like the dog in the photo. And that is why I wanted to write to you.

You see Roy, every time I hear you speak on the radio, it seems that you are angry or not satisfied with some aspect of life or with somebody you are working with. Fergal notices this especially – blind people have a great ear for these things. And this tone is at times bitter, sometimes sarcastic and other times fairly angry with the world. This makes me not like you very much. Why do you have to be so grumpy and dissatisfied? You are one of the luckiest Irish people ever, after winning so many great trophies and awards playing the sport you love. Fergal will not ever have these types of opportunities and all he knows of you is what he can hear. A lot of the time, what he hears isn't very pleasant.

But Roy, I have to say the picture shows a much nicer side to you. The dog in the picture looks so happy to be with you. You have a smile on your face and he wants to be in your company. Dogs have a great way of judging people. This photo tells me that deep down you have a nice, calm and friendly nature, just like the Labrador in the photo who is very like Jacko here in our house. He is 9 years old this year and is just as enthusiastic and careful as ever with Fergal. They know how people feel, they know when things are not right and they are great company, not just to those without eyesight but to people in general.

I have learned that your work with the Irish Guide Dogs Association has taken place over many years. I suspect that this work indicates a softer side to you, a side that I would like my brother Fergal to hear about much more often when we switch on the radio. It would be a great honour for us if we could one day meet up with you. I see that the Guide Dogs Association will be having a fundraiser in the Phoenix Park this July 16th. Myself and Fergal will be there, along with Jacko. Maybe it would be a nice time to meet up and we can share stories about

how tough life can be without sight and how important
it is to speak nicely to those less fortunate than ourselves.
Looking forward to your response.

All the best.

Yours sincerely,

James and Fergal Doyle (and Jacko the Guide Dog)

(523 words)

EXAMINER'S COMMENT

This is a creative and original response; the reference to the 'blind' family
member in response to a visual text is an excellent piece of creative thinking. It
does address the question asked and is structured/formatted like a letter, though
there is no address at the beginning. However, it does include a salutation and
appropriate conclusion. There are four decent paragraphs, each of which has a
distinct point within. Vocabulary and mechanics are good throughout. A high
scoring effort.

MARKS AWARDED

14 + 13 + 13 + 5 = 45/50 (O1 Grade)

Answer formats for B Questions

There is quite a variety in the B questions that could appear on your exam paper. Below
are some pointers for different formats you might use in your answers.

Newspaper articles

- **Read, read, read!** There is no substitute for reading newspapers regularly.
- **Tone**: When writing a newspaper article, decide immediately what the tone should
  be. Do you want it to be sincere, serious, light-hearted, sarcastic, angry, etc?
- **Headlines**: Tabloids tend to be more sensationalist than broadsheets, e.g. 'JAIL
  THE EVIL BEAST' as opposed to 'Killer to be sentenced tomorrow'. Tabloid
  headings can be very memorable. When Glasgow Celtic were beaten by Inverness
  Caledonian Thistle (a much smaller football team nicknamed 'Cally') the
  following headline appeared in a tabloid and reminded many people of *Mary
  Poppins*: 'SUPER-CALLY-GO-BALLISTIC-CELTIC-ARE-ATROCIOUS!!!'
- **Opening sentences**: All journalists are skilled at making an impact with their
  opening sentence.
- **Paragraph length**: Newspapers stick rigidly to one point per paragraph; words are
  not wasted.
- **Structure**: The most important information is placed at the start of the article.
  Lesser details are edited out or left to the end. This is called the 'upside-down
  pyramid' approach because readers frequently read only the start of an article.

- **Quotation**: Journalists use quotation carefully. When they are not sure of an exact quote, they paraphrase or use phrases like 'a source has indicated' or 'reports suggest that', etc.
- **Passive voice**: This means that an article should be written as if from a distance. The journalist does not let 'I' get in the way. They are not telling a story in the narrative sense; they report on what happened. For example: 'A bomb **was found** yesterday', rather than '**I heard** that there was a bomb'.

Reports

- Reports must be **factual** and free from excessive emotion.
- You could be asked to report on a traffic accident, sports event, talent show, report to a committee at the end of the year, etc.
- The most important thing to consider when writing a report is your **audience**. Who are you reporting to?
- Reports must be very **informative**.

Commentaries

- This question comes up occasionally. If you can copy the style of commentaries you hear on radio or TV, this is a possible choice.
- Commentaries require lots of emotion to communicate the excitement of an event. You will need to include some narration and information, but aesthetics should be your ultimate goal. Bring colour to the scene!
- Avoid cliché.
- Similar to tabloid newspaper headings, puns feature in commentaries:
  'It's snow joke: the race is being abandoned!'
  'It looks like curtains for Vladimir Karpets!'
  'John Carpenter nails his opponent!'
  'Woods is definitely in the trees!'
  'Keane to play no longer.'
  Try to include some funny puns in commentaries that you write.

Advertising

- This is all about selling and the clever use of images (in your case, words) to encourage people to buy a product.
- Information and persuasion are on show here.
- An advertisement needs a **slogan**: a catchy phrase to gain attention. Sometimes slogans are funny or even shocking.
- **Memorable information**: Advertisements use scientific or technical language, but they keep it to a minimum.

- **Buzzwords** include: 'best', 'unbeatable', 'superior' and 'a must'. Emotive sentences could be: 'Good parents always...'; 'Never, ever do...'; 'Could you possibly not...'; and 'You would be mad not to...'.
- **Repetition** is vital for product and brand recognition. Keep mentioning the product or the brand by name or by its benefit or result.

Talks

- In many ways, this is the least formal of all the writing exercises in the exam.
- Once again, you must consider your audience.
- It is likely that this question will ask you to write a talk to be given to some of your **peers** or **colleagues**. Therefore, use the register (vocabulary, tone, purpose, etc.) that you would use when speaking to peers or friends. Practise this in class.
- When writing informal content, it is still important to avoid excessive **slang** or phrases that are too casual, vague or loose.

> - like - really - kind of - sort of - yeah - nah - mate - dude - bud

exam focus

Choose the Comprehension B Question that you like most by determining the task involved and the type of writing that is required.

5 Composition

- To analyse the **types of questions** that are found in the Composition section of the exam.
- To demonstrate the key differences between **story** and **discussion** questions.
- To understand the importance of **planning** in this section.

- The Composition section accounts for 25 per cent of the entire exam.
- This part of the exam will take you about **80 minutes** in total.
- Aim to write anything from **700 words upwards**.
- However, the old saying of '**quality not quantity**' applies here.
- Quality essay writing is dependent on good planning, so this aspect is covered in detail later on in this chapter.

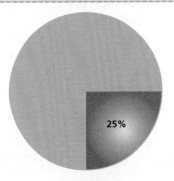

25%

key point

Breakdown of the Composition section:

- The paper contains **seven** composition titles.
- Students choose **one**: worth **100 marks** in total.
- Exam papers from the last number of years reveal that the titles given allow for a choice between a type of **story** and a type of **discussion**, or a combination of both.
- There is sometimes an option to write a **personal essay** based on the visuals in the Comprehension section in Paper 1. Pay attention to the visuals when reading the questions.

If you want to write a talk, speech or article for your Composition, use the guidelines in Chapter 4 for Comprehension B questions. However, remember that your **Composition answer must be longer!**

PAST COMPOSITION QUESTIONS

2017

1. Write a **short story** which features a character who gets into trouble because of his or her sense of humour.

2. Imagine that you have been selected as the Student of the Year in your school and have been asked to deliver a **speech to the staff and students at a school assembly**. The topic for your speech is 'My School Days'. Write the speech, which may be serious or humorous or both, that you would deliver.

3. Imagine you find a box of items from your childhood in your parents' attic. Write a **personal essay** in which you identify what you find in the box and describe the feelings and memories these items evoke for you.

4. Write a **short story** in which a family comes to regret adopting a robot.

5. You have been asked to write an **article for a magazine** popular with young people. In your article you should give advice to Leaving Certificate students on how to develop their study skills, maintain a healthy lifestyle while preparing for exams, and balance study with the more social aspects of life.

6. Write a **personal essay** giving your views on the importance of praise and encouragement as we go through life.

7. Imagine you are a robot teacher. Write at least **three diary entries** in which you record your impressions of humans in general, write specifically about your work as a teacher and give your views on the behaviour of the students that you teach. Your diary entries may be humorous or serious or both.

2016

1. Write a **personal essay** about the pleasures of life's lazy days.

2. Write a **short story** in which the main character goes on an exciting journey and learns some valuable lessons along the way.

3. Imagine that it is the year 3016 and you are living in a city on Mars. Write **three diary entries** in which you describe the world in which you live, give details of your daily life and your hopes for the future.

4. Write a **personal essay** about your own experience of any two of the following: kindness; patience; generosity; tolerance and forgiveness.

5. Write an **article for a travel magazine**, in which you encourage young people to visit Ireland, telling them why they should come here, and what you recommend they should see and do during their visit.

6. Write a **short story** which features two characters who hold opposing points of view.

7. Write a **speech**, to be delivered to your class, in which you talk about at least one occasion in your life when you were glad you persevered with something.

2015

1. Write a **short story** in which one character deceives another.
2. Write an **article for your school magazine**, in which you explain why you love reading; discuss some of the books that you have most enjoyed and encourage everybody to read more.
3. Write a **personal essay** about an occasion when you overcame opposition to do something you believed to be important.
4. Write an **article for a popular magazine** entitled, 'My Passion for Fashion'.
5. Imagine you are a representative of the Irish Society for the Prevention of Cruelty to Animals (ISPCA). Write a **speech**, to be delivered in schools, in which you explain the practicalities and responsibilities involved in keeping a pet and encourage the students in your audience to treat animals with respect.
6. Write a **personal essay** in which you reflect on various significant losses in your life.
7. Write a **short story** in which one or more modern devices make life difficult for the character or characters in the story.

Once you have chosen your question, you will most likely be writing one of the following types of composition:

- Short story.
- Personal essay: A story or discussion based on your own experience. The 'I' voice is important here.
- Talk or speech to an audience.
- An article of some sort, e.g. newspaper, magazine, blog, etc.

Spend some time **browsing** these and other essay titles. Make a note of the titles you would prefer and those you would prefer to avoid. This is the first step in choosing a title and properly planning your essays.

The Composition question is sometimes referred to as the 'essay question'. Some students are intimidated by the thoughts of writing such an essay. It may indeed be the longest piece of continuous writing you have ever written. Over the years, some preconceived notions about the Composition question have taken hold. Let's tackle them here.

key point

It is a serious error in the exam to choose a story or a personal experience essay if that is not where your strengths lie.

1. **'You can write a short story or essay without any planning.'**
   False

   A certain amount of imagination and creativity is needed here. But it is also very difficult to do this question without some sort of plan beforehand. Spider diagrams, mind maps, scribbled notes or whatever suits you will definitely help in creating the final product in the exam. Practice this beforehand; also spend about 10–15 minutes in the exam itself planning what you will write. This is time well spent. It will give structure or shape to your answer. This is what examiners are looking for. **It is obvious that planning and practice before the exam is vital.**

2. **'Writing a story is always the best option.'**
   False

   This issue is of huge significance. While it may seem easy to write a story, other options such as a speech, magazine article or personal essay may suit certain candidates better. If you are not a good storyteller, you will still have plenty of options on the day.

   It is important that you work with your teacher to determine if you have adequate storytelling skills. Otherwise, avoid the short story options and concentrate on something else. Look back over some Leaving Certificate short stories and see if they inspire you to write your own story.

3. **'The essay will decide if you get an A grade or not, or if the examiner will pass or fail you.'**
   Partly True

   Given that this question comprises 25 per cent of the entire exam, it does have a major bearing on your overall grade. However, it is marked according to strict criteria and examiners are trained to look for particular qualities and features. They are not out to judge your opinions or views; they need to examine your language skills.

4. **'Personal, unique, original essays get automatic A grades.'**
   False

   Perhaps you have heard of some famous A1 essays, such as the one entitled 'Creation', where a candidate drew a map of the world. Or an essay entitled 'Why?', for which the candidate wrote 'Why not?'. Or best of all, the one about 'Bravery', which inspired a bright student to hand up four blank pages. What grade did they all receive? Such efforts obviously get zero! A good student will aim for anything from **700 words upwards**, which amounts to roughly **two and a half or three A4 pages at a bare minimum.**

5. **'You can learn off an essay and twist it to suit any exercise.'**
   Possible – But not at all advisable

   Some teachers have suggested this approach. However, there is the possibility that the student will fail to answer the question asked, which is one of the main reasons for poor grades in English. Unoriginal, 'learned-off' essays do not score well. You can, of course, use an essay plan or outline that went well for you during the year, provided that you follow what the essay question asks of you in the actual exam.

6. **'The Composition is the most important question of the entire exam.'**
   Partly True

Again, with 25 per cent on the line, this is an area to which students must devote time and practice. It is also worth reminding you that no amount of practice and preparation can account for simply writing a bad essay on the day. However, if you make some good choices and write to your full potential, you should be fine.

key point

It's all in the plan!

Option 1: A short story

Planning

As rugby pundit George Hook once said, rule number one for making chicken soup is to catch the chicken! The same applies to writing a short story composition. Catch the chicken by making a **sensible, coherent plan**:

- **Underline key words and jot down ideas.** This applies to all questions on the paper, but the composition is mostly about **your own ideas and expression**, so try to think broadly about the topic once you have underlined the key words.

- **Spend at least 15 minutes planning the detail.** All planning begins with **brainstorming**. It can take the form of spider diagrams or mind maps – whatever way you can comfortably get your thoughts on the page. You may scribble single words or draw diagrams; it really does not matter once you have a way of doing it. Then connect the ideas by following the pointers below.

- The **narrative voice** of a story is important. Pick one of these options:
  1. I am in the story, telling it. This is a **first person narrative**.
  2. I am outside the story, telling it. An 'all-seeing' narrator is used in a **third person narrative**.

exam focus

Remember that first person narratives don't have to be true to life. Invent a story about yourself. You can be anybody!

Key ingredients for a good short story

- Have a **small number of characters**: two or three characters with one main character or **protagonist**. When planning, create a quick profile of each character, listing gender, age, features, etc.

- Give each personality **one strong trait**, such as: aggression; impatience; humour; an unusual talent; unique features, etc.

- Work within a **narrow timeframe**. The hub of your story could take place in a few hours or one single day, with a significant episode.

- Include **dialogue** and interaction. Use these elements to suggest details to the reader, e.g. the setting, time and location.

- In order to interest your reader, there must be a challenge, obstacle or **conflict** that the main character must overcome. All good stories contain conflict.
- There must be **tension** or uncertainty before your conflict is resolved. Situations in real life rarely run smoothly; when they do, they make for boring stories.
- Know the **ending** before you begin.
- Understand the purpose of stories. Aim to entertain and **engage** the reader. If the story bores you, it will bore the reader, too.
- Remember the **audience** for your story. In this case, it will be the examiner.
- Do not be at all inhibited or shy about expressing yourself. Speak from the well of your own experiences. Be creative!

Bad planning

To demonstrate how things can go wrong without a plan, read the following passage from a student who chose Question 2 from the 2006 exam. It asks for a short story ending with the sentence: 'What a relief!' The student wrote the entire essay without any planning. So many problems are demonstrated in just this opening paragraph. See if you can identify these weaknesses yourself before reading the analysis overleaf.

What a relief!

Five best friends spent months planning their dream vacation trying to find the perfect place with a mixture of nights out, a relaxing atmosphere during the day and a place you would only go once in a lifetime. John was a typical teenager and loved nothing more than going out with his friends. He was tall and strong and a gym fanatic. He was nineteen years old. John's four best friends were the same age as him and they were friends since playschool. Despite what most people thought, John's friends were not as bad as they seemed. They were party animals and always went out any chance they had, drinking and taking as much drugs as they could get into them. They decided to go to Bangkok in Thailand for six weeks.

Analysis of sample paragraph

This opening paragraph reads like an essay disaster waiting to happen.

- In a short story, you have little time to develop characters. Choose two or three at most. This student has included **far too many characters** for a short story composition.
- Try to avoid **common names** like John or Mary. Go for something more memorable.
- **Personalities** are important. Why does John have to be a 'typical teenager'? Surely it is more interesting to read about a character that is unusual or unique. Also, few nineteen-year-olds fit the bill as 'typical teenagers'.
- Timeframe is crucial. This paragraph suggests that the action will cover a total of six weeks. This is **far too long a timeframe** for this kind of composition. It is better

to write short episodes covering a day in the life – even a few minutes in the lives – of a small number of characters.

- The **content** is rather clichéd. The story of five young males heading to Thailand for six weeks has been told so many times. Given the title, it is quite likely that the boys will: have a brush with the law; dabble in drink, drugs, sex or a combination of them all; and somehow escape with their lives only to exclaim, 'What a relief!' This storyline is unoriginal, predictable and lacks imagination. If it was a film, you wouldn't bother watching it.

- Other storylines that are overdone include:
  - **Scoring the winning goal in a football final.**
  - **Waking up to discover that 'it was all a dream'.**
  - **Describing complicated intimate relationships between boyfriends and girlfriends.**
  - **Killing off the narrator at the end. This seldom makes sense in the context of a story.**
  - **Any type of clichéd, overused storylines involving: drinking, drugs, parties, pregnancies, the police, etc.**

While there might be some merit in these subject areas, the problem is that they tend not to be very interesting or **original**. Examiners feel that they have heard all of these stories before and so they will not score them highly in the exam. Therefore, **don't write about them**, unless the question specifically asks you to.

- Given the title, the ending for this story is of huge importance. In fact, **the ending is crucial in all stories** and students should know the end before they begin to write. This title suggests a happy ending: John probably escapes with his life. But perhaps the final phrase could be the words of the police-chief in Thailand who is delighted to put John behind bars for his drug-trafficking crimes. It is up to you to determine the ending. Just make sure you decide on it before you begin to write.

- We have examined the **content** problems with this sample paragraph. However, there are also **style** issues to be considered. **How** the story is written (vocabulary, sentence structure, grammar, etc.) accounts for another 40 per cent of the marks. Clearly there are style problems in this sample paragraph also: the **opening sentence** is too long; the **vocabulary** is limited; and overall there is not much to recommend it.

exam focus

Include any rough work or planning you did with your answer booklet. Examiners do take note of this material.

key point

The opening paragraph is the most important paragraph to get right.

SAMPLE SHORT STORY

 exam Q

Q. 1.

Write a short story which features a character who gets into trouble because of his or her sense of humour.

- This was the essay title no.1 on the 2017 paper. It is a straightforward concept that presents lots of imaginative potential.
- Many of us can relate to this concept. Think of a real life story where this happened.
- Plan your essay by brainstorming or using mind maps or diagrams to work out how your story will develop.

key point

If an essay title immediately sticks out as being familiar or close to your own personal experience, then it is likely a good choice in the exam.

Here is a sample brainstorming diagram:

Brainstorming

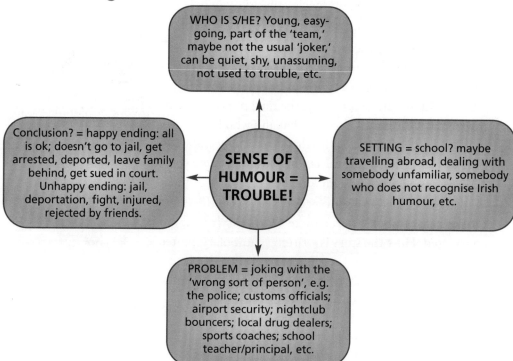

WHO IS S/HE? Young, easy-going, part of the 'team,' maybe not the usual 'joker,' can be quiet, shy, unassuming, not used to trouble, etc.

Conclusion? = happy ending: all is ok; doesn't go to jail, get arrested, deported, leave family behind, get sued in court. Unhappy ending: jail, deportation, fight, injured, rejected by friends.

SENSE OF HUMOUR = TROUBLE!

SETTING = school? maybe travelling abroad, dealing with somebody unfamiliar, somebody who does not recognise Irish humour, etc.

PROBLEM = joking with the 'wrong sort of person', e.g. the police; customs officials; airport security; nightclub bouncers; local drug dealers; sports coaches; school teacher/principal, etc.

Short Story – Outline

Having spent 5–10 minutes brainstorming on blank paper, you should now put together the 'shell' of your story. It should have a defined setting, in a time and place, have a clear beginning, middle and end and a sense that a short time passes. It should be realistic enough and you absolutely **must** know how it will end before you start writing.

Here is a suggestion:

> As a group of friends are returning from a trip to America, one of them tries to joke that he has a bomb in his hand luggage. This does not go down well at all and only after being questioned by airport police are they let go home. But they miss their flight and the friends are not entirely happy.

Beginning/Introduction

'Show', don't 'Tell'

Your opening paragraph is vital. It is better to 'hint' and 'suggest' at a time and place, rather than just listing details.

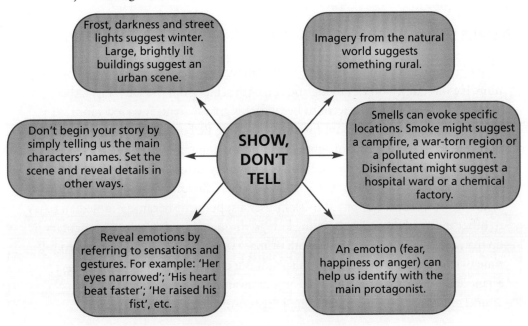

Have a read of this opening paragraph:

> I don't like airports at the best of times. There is something about the waiting around, the crowds, the over-priced food and the hustle and bustle that just wears me out. Yes, I love the adventure of travelling, the excitement of seeing friends and relatives abroad, the thought of unexplored lands to be conquered. It's the getting through the airport bit that I dread most. Plus, it's hard enough having to

mentally deal with things like bombers and terrorists on the news every night. So when Shane decided for some ungodly and outrageous reason to start some funny small talk with the pretty security guard, I knew we were going to be here for a bit longer than usual.

At this stage, we have:

- Setting (airport)
- Characters: narrator, Shane, security guard. This is enough.
- Problem/Obstacle (trouble with security)
- Lots of possibilities from which to develop the story

Middle/Main body of the story

We now need to engage the reader/examiner with some character details. Given the time constraints of the exam, we can't tell the whole life story of anybody – so choose some strong trait that will make the character interesting.

Example: Shane = **confident, funny, amusing**. Likes to entertain people. This is what causes the problem.

SAMPLE PARAGRAPH

I have been friends with Shane since he first moved to the countryside when he was nine. He was quirky, quick-talking and full of mischief from the start. His father and mother had separated so he went to live with his grandparents for a few months to help him cope. They lived about fifty miles south of Belfast City, just over the old border in what is County Monaghan, right next to our family farm. 'Patrick Kavanagh Country' they called it with its stony, grey, drumlin soil. It may as well have been a different continent to a lad like Shane, who knew nothing but life in a terraced West Belfast row of red-brick houses. I suppose he became a comedian to try to offset the usual turmoil that young kids go through. His quick-fire commentary lit up many a boring day in the two-room primary school, once his mother moved full time to live with him the following autumn. But enough of the pop psychology: Shane and I were now stuck in JFK Airport, awaiting what we were told was 'homeland security protocol' after one-joke-too-many from dear old Shane.

At this stage:

- We now know more about the characters and their relationship.
- We are heading towards a climax or turning point or 'key moment' that needs to be resolved.
- We are continuing to 'hint' and 'show' the reader our story – details are gradually revealed.
- We need **dialogue** to take the story further.

SAMPLE PARAGRAPH – USING DIALOGUE

It is best to end this story on a positive note, otherwise it will be too long and involve too many extra characters, i.e. security guards, lawyers, embassy officials, parents etc. To keep it simple, we will imagine the discussion that might occur between Shane, the narrator (whose name will be revealed in the dialogue) and an airport security official, as they are being released from custody.

My cheap, two-dollar plastic watch was holding up better than me and reminded me that we were now four hours here and our flight long gone. The door marked 'Airport Security – No Unauthorised Entrance' suddenly swung open and a grim-faced Shane strode out awkwardly, rubbing his wrists as he did so.

'Those wee handcuffs were pure unnecessary,' he whispered to me as we stood together, 'and too tight for my liking. Think I'm some kinda wacko bomber nutjob or something. Pure madness.'

Before we could exchange any more particulars, an equally grim-faced security guard interrupted us as she swished through the door just behind Shane. It was then that I noticed her name tag: **Julia Alvarez – Department of Homeland Security**. Christ, for a moment I thought I was in a TV show.

'Ok you guys, I know Irish people can be funny,' she began in a sharp, pointed tone, 'but in the United States, all persons suspected of, or known to be accomplices of known enemies to the peace of this nation, or any other freedom-loving country, is given the level of attention necessary to establish their likeliness to do harm to themselves or others while in the country. We don't make jokes about being bombers or terrorists. Do you understand the seriousness of the situation here?' I was exhausted trying to work out what that long sentence actually meant. But I think the penny had dropped with Shane.

'Yes, Julia... I mean Miss Alvarez, I sure do,' he nodded solemnly, trying not to wink at her as he was fond of doing. 'I was only having a wee laugh, pulling yer ould leg if ya know what I mean.' She apparently did not enjoy the thought of an 18-year-old sunburnt, Irish Paddy pulling her leg or indeed anybody else's. I intervened on our behalf.

'Thank you, Miss Alvarez. Shane is a good friend of mine. I know him for years and we have never been in any trouble whatsoever. You can check that with the authorities in Ireland.' I'm sure she had already. I was putting on my very best innocent, wide-eyed altar-boy face. She still wasn't impressed.

'Well, thank you, Mr Callahan, but we have looked into both your affairs and thankfully you appear to have a clean record.' It was the first bit of relief I had felt that evening. But Julia wasn't finished: 'For now!' she added gravely, with a sullen stare at Shane.

CONCLUDING PARAGRAPH

Since this is a positive ending, we want something to tie it together, to have something that the examiner will see merit in.

> We were handed back our passports, our luggage was thrown at our feet and with that, we were free to go again. No longer suspected terrorists with bombs in our luggage but just two teenage Irish lads again, heading home from our weekend break to New York, courtesy of Aunt Mary living in Queens. But Julia Alvarez had the last word:
>
> 'Mr Callahan. Ah, is your name really Harry Callahan?' The question made me pause for a second. Of course it was my name. Did she think I was on a fake passport now or what?
>
> 'Yes. That's my name. Is everything ok?' I enquired nervously.
>
> 'It's fine. Ya know, maybe you should head to San Francisco next time. You can tell them Dirty Harry is back. They might actually find that funny.'
>
> For the first time she actually smiled. Shane, not being much of a movie fan, shrugged his shoulders, lifted his bag and strode off towards the terminal, a free man once again. I was glad to follow. This time, we were both keeping our mouths shut.

- This conclusion reveals the narrator's full name.
- It is a light-hearted ending to a serious scenario.
- We can see differences in each of the characters' attitudes at this point of the story.
- It ties up the plot in a short timescale and involves a limited number of characters.
- Dialogue is used once more to make the story sound realistic.

Option 2: A personal essay

The personal essay asks you to write about an experience you had. Thankfully, it involves **planning** that is broadly similar to the short story. The main difference is that it is expected to be more **sincere** than an imaginative story.

You must be wary of some common pitfalls. Students sometimes write about experiences that are simply not very interesting. Or sometimes they express an opinion that is not thought out fully or is badly informed, in spite of their personal experiences. Examples of themes that are sometimes poorly dealt with include racism, world politics and relationships.

Improving the personal essay option

You should follow all of the advice given for planning a story. When you read an essay title, ask yourself if you have knowledge or experience of it. Do you hold strong opinions on the topic? **If you are unsure, don't choose this particular essay title.**

Being clear about **purpose**, **audience** and **register** (PAR) is an essential skill for doing Paper 1. It is particularly important when it comes to the personal essay question.

Purpose

Ask yourself what your essay aims to achieve. If you intend to describe paradise, as one of the essay options of 2008 asked, your essay must be one that would genuinely appeal to any reader. It must be convincing. You will have to include the **language of persuasion**, along with some **narration** and **aesthetics.**

Audience

Consider who you are writing the essay for. Obviously the examiner will read your essay, but you should write with the presumption that it could be read and appreciated by others. Therefore, you should imagine that you are writing for someone you can trust. Think of your reader as someone who won't judge you, but is **interested in hearing you say something interesting**.

Register

Remember that register involves many elements. It requires: specific **vocabulary**; appropriate **tone**; and proper **treatment of the task** at hand.

It is helpful to fill out a **PAR plan** before you write a personal essay. Examine the plan for 'My Idea of Paradise' below.

My Idea of Paradise		
Purpose	**Audience**	**Register**
• To show that I have a clear idea of the concept: paradise. • To describe clearly my version of paradise.	• Friends who would understand me. • People who would not ridicule my view, but ask questions about it. • The examiner, who will grade my effort.	• Sincere: it needs to sound like I really mean it. • Light-hearted: since it is a pleasant topic. • Convincing: I need to explain myself well and convince the examiner of my point of view.

Personal essay based on visuals (Pictures)

- If you decide to write a personal essay in response to the visuals on your exam paper, be very sure about your choice. If you **like reading visual texts**, then a personal essay based on visuals might be the perfect choice for you. For a reminder of how to respond to visuals, look at Chapter 4, pp. 27–30 and follow the advice found there.

Clarity and coherence

The Composition section is a tremendous test of your vocabulary and expression. There are many tips and language aids available for this question. However, the most important thing to remember is the need for **clarity and coherence**:

- Have **clear ideas** in your head. Think before you write!
- Write **coherent sentences**. This means keeping things simple and understandable.

You cannot go far wrong if you keep these things in mind.

Sentences

Below is some useful information about sentences:

- Each sentence must have a **subject**, i.e. something doing the action.
  Example: The **Shannon** is the longest river in Ireland.
- Each sentence must have a **verb**, i.e. the action word.
  Example: The Shannon **flows** through the midlands.
- Each sentence must be a **complete thought**.
- If one or more of these elements is missing, then you have a **phrase**, rather than a sentence.
  Examples: – flows through the midlands (no subject)
     – longest river in Ireland (no subject or verb)
- Using phrases rather than complete sentences can lead to lower quality writing. Always ensure your sentences contain: a subject, a verb and a complete thought.
- Sentences can become more complex, but if you **read** and **write** a lot you will gain confidence in structuring them.

Improving your expression

A **dictionary** or **thesaurus** can be very useful in improving your expression and adding depth to your sentences. Here is an example of a simple sentence:

The Shannon flows through the midlands.

This is a basic sentence using informative language. See how it changes when we add some **adjectives**. Adjectives are descriptive words used to modify nouns.

*The **majestic, sparkling** Shannon flows through the **lush, flat** midland region of Ireland.*

We can also include **adverbs**. Adverbs are descriptive words used to modify verbs.

*The majestic, sparking Shannon flows **lazily** through the lush, flat midland region of Ireland.*

We can even add new **phrases** or **clauses**.

*The majestic, sparkling Shannon, **Ireland's longest river,** flows lazily through the lush, flat midland region of the country.*

Notice how the extra clause is added; it is separated with commas. See how the end of the sentence is tweaked to avoid repetition. 'Region of Ireland' has become 'region of the country' to avoid repetition of the word 'Ireland'.

Paragraphs

A paragraph contains a series of sentences that are linked by the same theme or idea. Here are some tips on using paragraphs:

- Become comfortable with paragraphs by practising your essays regularly. All good compositions are paragraphed well.
- Start a new paragraph when you want to move to: a new point; a new location; a new idea; a new speaker; new dialogue; or when you want to conclude your essay.
- Paragraphs are strongly advised in exam answers because they show that you have put order and structure on your work.
- Even if you are not entirely certain, begin a new paragraph if you feel you should. Paragraphs always look better on the page than a big, solid block of text.

key point

Paragraphs are not optional!

Tips for avoiding some common pitfalls

- Aim for the *right* word, rather than a big word that you may not be able to use correctly.
- Regularly read a **thesaurus** to increase your vocabulary.
- Verbs, adjectives and adverbs should be varied as much as possible to breathe life and colour into your work.
- The composition might not actually be all about 'you', so try to avoid starting too many sentences with 'I' or having too many references to 'me'. Try thinking outside of yourself and try to see things from other points of view.
- Writing good **comedy** is considered very challenging because we all have a different sense of what we find funny. Seek advice from teachers or classmates beforehand. See if you have a gift for humorous writing. It might be a talent you can use in the exam.
- Stick to the task always. Answer the question asked. Be decisive and confident in your writing and don't write down that you 'don't know' things. Examiners want to reward what you know, not punish you for not knowing.

Meaningless words

'Verbiage' is a great word for what is also called waffle! This occurs when we include unnecessary words or when we use words that carry little or no meaning. Look at some examples below:

Smile *on his face* (Where else would it be?)

Few *in number* (Few already indicates a number.)

Past history (History is in the past.)

Very unique (Unique means one of a kind. There is no such thing as 'very unique'.)

Rectangular *shape* (A rectangle is a shape.)

Meet *together* ('Meet' means coming together.)

Small *in size* ('Small' indicates size.)

General public (Is there a non-general public?)

If you read quality newspapers and books, you will avoid verbiage and you will understand and appreciate good writing.

Words and expressions to be avoided!

The following expressions do not exist:	**The following expressions do exist, but they are used far too often!**
<ul><li>Could of</li><li>Would of</li><li>Might of</li><li>Should of</li></ul>	<ul><li>Sort of</li><li>You know</li><li>Like</li></ul>

key point

If you use coarse or vulgar language in your Leaving Certificate exam, your final grade will be seriously affected.

Emphatic words

When you use too many emphatic words, you imply that what you're saying is absolute fact and is not open to argument.

The following emphatic words should be used carefully:

- Always
- Never
- All
- None
- Total
- Complete
- Absolute
- Entire

Hyperbole

Hyperbole is pronounced 'hi-per-boh-lay' and means gross exaggeration. To describe Yeats as the 'greatest, most outstanding, supreme poet in any language whatsoever' might fit your beliefs, but it would be more measured to say: 'I admire Yeats for the following reasons...'

Clichés

Try to avoid clichéd phrases. Use the table below to improve your writing. On the left are some particularly clichéd phrases. Think of original ways of expressing these same ideas and write your new phrases on the right.

A game of two halves	
Raining cats and dogs	
Daylight robbery	
Pure class	
Going forward	
In the current climate	
The writing is on the wall	
As black as coal	
As cold as ice	
As red as blood	
As blue as the sea	
As dark as night	
As white as snow	
At the end of the day	
Backs to the wall	
In this day and age	
Ordinary man in the street	
Leave no stone unturned	
Openness and transparency	
Cool, calm and collected	
To be sure	
A terrible tragedy	
Sight for sore eyes	
Knee high to a grasshopper	
Coming on leaps and bounds	

You might have to use clichés on occasion and the examiner might not penalise you too much for them. However, the whole idea of the exam is to test your expression. So think creatively and aim for originality!

The Single Text

- To outline key points to remember for Single Text revision.
- To identify the typical questions that could be asked in this section.
- To examine some texts in detail to show how to revise.

Getting started

- You will have studied **ONE** text in detail for this part of the exam.
- The questions will be quite specific.
- The writing tasks are sometimes like those found in the comprehensions on Paper 1.
- There are 60 marks available – so spend around 55 minutes on this section.

15%

2018 Exam

- **BRONTË, Emily** *Wuthering Heights*
- **FITZGERALD, F. Scott** *The Great Gatsby*
- **MILLER, Arthur** *All My Sons*
- **NGOZI ADICHIE, Chimamanda** *Americanah*
- **SHAKESPEARE, William** *King Lear*
- **BINCHY, Maeve** *Circle of Friends*
- **GAIMAN, Neil** *The Ocean at the End of the Lane*
- **O'CASEY, Sean** *The Plough and the Stars*
- **RYAN, Donal** *The Spinning Heart*

2019 Exam

- **AUSTEN, Jane** *Persuasion*
- **ATWOOD, Margaret** *The Handmaid's Tale*
- **CARR, Marina** *By the Bog of Cats*
- **NGOZI ADICHIE, Chimamanda** *Americanah*
- **SHAKESPEARE, William** *Macbeth*
- **DONOGHUE, Emma** *Room*

There are several questions/exam pages in Paper 2 that are of no relevance to you on the day. Identify your chosen 'Single Text' and ignore the others.

- **FITZGERALD, F. Scott** *The Great Gatsby*
- **RYAN, Donal** *The Spinning Heart*
- **SYNGE, J. M.** *The Playboy of the Western World*

Revising the Single Text – WARNING!

The first thing to do here is to be **sure which text you have studied for the Single Text question.** This cannot be stressed enough for each student.

- You cannot then use that same text again in any other section.
- You will be severely penalised for using the same text again in the exam.

> **key point**
>
> You must know the difference between the 'Single Text' and 'Comparative Texts' before the exam starts. Each school and teacher will make different choices.

Answering questions

When answering exam questions, your answers should follow a familiar format:

POINT – QUOTE – EXPLAIN OR 'P.Q.E.'

This means that you must **write something**, include supporting **quotes or references** and then follow things up with some **further explanation of your own**.

Examiners will be on the look-out for this approach to answers on Paper 2 especially.

Question format

60 marks in total

- **Three 10-mark questions – Do all three – 30 minutes**
- **Three longer 30-mark questions – Do ONE – 25 minutes**

10-mark questions

- Comment on **specific moments** or issues in the text.
- Comment on a **specific character** and their role in the text.
- Your answers should be **precise. Stick to what the question asks.** You should write 6 or 7 full sentences and address the question directly with your opening sentence.

> **key point**
>
> You must use your time wisely so always remember the number of marks per question.

- Follow the **'statement–quotation–comment'** approach; i.e. say something to begin with, include a quote or reference, then finish with a follow-up comment.
- Spend a maximum of 10 minutes on each answer and no more than **30 minutes in total for these three questions.**
- If you are running out of time, **finish what you are doing and move on** – there are many more sections to come.

30-mark questions

Since there are **30 marks** available, spend no more than **25 minutes** on this question. This includes writing a **short plan or brainstorm before you begin.** These are the types of questions that you should **practice beforehand when studying.**

Typical tasks

- Take a **personal point of view** on a theme/issue in the studied text.
- Imagine that you are 'character x' and write an **account of a key moment.**
- **Write a journalistic article** of some sort based upon the events of the studied text.
- **Write a diary/journal entry** of a key character.
- **Write a letter** to/from a character from the text.

> The writing skills needed on Paper 1 are just as important in Paper 2.

Selected Single Texts

There are some essential areas for revision of the Single Text. These are:

- STORYLINE – what happens?
- MAIN CHARACTERS – who does what and why?
- MAIN THEMES and ISSUES – what does the text teach us?

There is a total of fifteen different 'Single Texts' available for study in the 2018 and 2019 Leaving Cert exam years. We will concentrate on **six of the more popular texts** suggested for Ordinary Level students.

- *The Spinning Heart* (2018/19)
- *The Great Gatsby* (2018/19)
- *The Plough and the Stars* (2018)
- *The Playboy of the Western World* (2018)
- *Room* (2019)
- *Circle of Friends* (2019)

1. *The Spinning Heart* by Donal Ryan (2018/19)

Storyline

- *The Spinning Heart* is set in an unnamed rural Irish village during **the severe economic crisis** from 2008 onwards that followed the Celtic Tiger years.
- It consists of **twenty-one separate first-person accounts** of how life has panned out for everyone in this **desolate*** and **depressing** place.

- The story is a **testimony*** of the **collapse of normality in people's everyday lives**, especially within the **family unit**. It started when a 'young Cunliffe lad' was shot dead by the armed-response unit. His old aunt then sold off the land to allow Pokey Burke to begin his building spree.

- Bobby Mahon is the first character to speak in the novel. We learn of his hatred towards his father. **'I go there every day to see is he dead and every day he lets me down.'** This sentence sets the tone for much of the novel as many dark and unpleasant experiences are remembered.

- We must piece together the story from all these chapters. However, a small number of characters play a major part in the action. These are:
    — **Pokey Burke** (he does not have a chapter – others speak about him)
    — **Bobby**
    — **Triona**
    — **Frank**
    — **Denis**
    — **Josie**
    — **Realtin**
    — **Trevor**

- The main **villain** of the story is the 'cowboy' builder and developer **Pokey Burke**. However, he does not speak at all. He is the villain because his failure to properly look after so many people employed by him has led to many of the financial and family problems and the **demise*** in general in the town. Many of the other characters then **tell their own story,** seeing reflections of their own lives in the events tied to Pokey and the various associated local people.

- The local small-town hero of sorts, **Bobby Mahon,** Pokey's **handsome but volatile*** young foreman, is suspected of murdering his **bitter and vindictive*** father, **Frank**. However, this is not true, as it was **Denis** who did so in a fit of rage one evening. Bobby's wife **Triona** provides us with an important chapter outlining the 'real' Bobby, a person quite different to his public image. She also dismisses the idea that Bobby is having an affair with **Realtin**, putting it down to gossip.

- Midway through, Realtin's baby is kidnapped from a crèche, causing all sorts of panic. The kidnapper is **Trevor**, a mentally unstable Montessori teacher and friend of the equally disturbed young man, Lloyd. The baby is rescued, unharmed, following a tip-off from young **Timmy** who informed **Jim**, the local Garda Sergeant.

- The book concludes with a long and thoughtful chapter from **Triona**, who asks us: 'what matters only love?'

CHARACTERS

Each of the twenty-one characters has something interesting to say about themselves or somebody else. Each chapter contains some **key words or a quotation** that is central to their perspective. Here are some suggestions:

Bobby – a central character in the story, he is married to Triona and was Pokey Burke's foreman and the local town hero, despite being quite insecure and full of self-doubt: '**Imagine being so suddenly useless.**'

Josie – he is the father of Pokey, who tries to explain in his own head why Pokey became the man that he is: '**Who's to blame when a child turns rotten?**'

Lily – she is described by the locals as 'the bike', a crude reference to her status as the local prostitute: '**Like the men that came to my door, nature overpowers me.**'

Vasya – he is from Khakassia in Siberia, an immigrant worker cheated by Pokey: '**I took from others words and phrases that served me well for a while:** *off the books, under the table, on the queue tee.*'

Realtin – she is an attractive but fickle young single mother living in a near-empty, half-built housing estate, who has a fancy for Bobby Mahon: '**There's nobody living in the other houses, just the ghosts of people who never existed.**'

Timmy – he is a vulnerable yet likeable young labourer whose mother died giving birth to him: '**Bobby was always fair sound to me. He was the only one never slagged me.**'

Brian – he has just left school and sees very little future for himself in Ireland: '**I won't think about Lorna again once I start tapping some fine blondie wan below in Australia, that's what I'm getting at.**'

Trevor – he comes from a family with a history of mental illness and domestic troubles. He is a Montessori teacher but with a disturbing personality: '**I'm dying. I'm sure of it. One day soon my heart will just stop dead.**'

Bridie – she has never recovered from the tragic drowning of her beloved son twenty years earlier: '**How is it at all that I let one child take my whole heart? It wasn't fair on anyone. Life isn't fair as the fella says.**'

Jason – he is an abuse victim who is also a casual witness to the murder of Frank without realising it: **'The very minute you have a tattoo on your face the whole world looks at you different.'**

Hillary – she is a work colleague and a two-faced 'friend' of Realtin: **'A lot of those culchies are mad though. They're so *repressed* like. They all spend their whole lives going to mass and playing GAA and eating farm animals and cabbage.'**

Seanie – he is father to Realtin's child, although they don't enjoy a close relationship: **'I was always a pure solid madman for women. I couldn't stop thinking about them from when I was a small boy.'**

Denis – he is the one who actually kills Frank, in a fit of rage one evening, due to extreme stress: **'I haven't a snowball's chance in hell of a job. I'm owed a small fortune. The sky is falling down.'**

Kate – she is married to Denis. She runs the local crèche and when the economic crash occurs her business suffers: **'One good thing that happened since the recession started is that people will work for less than the minimum wage.'**

Lloyd – he claims to be a solipsist, a nonsense-philosophy that believes the entire universe consists of just him and his thoughts. He is an associate of Trevor who conspires in the kidnapping of Realtin's child from the crèche: **'I dreamt I killed the kid. That kind of fucked things up, I can tell you.'**

Rory – he is a sensitive young man who is crippled by self-doubts and a lack of confidence: **'Every bollocks is going around cribbing about the country being fucked. It'd wear you out so it would.'**

Millicent – she is a small child who likes to copy her parents' angry outbursts and practises her daddy's bad language: **'Mammy works in Tesco's. She told Daddy that she has to work her fingers to the bone. I cried when I heard Mammy say that.'**

Mags – she is the sister of Pokey. She is a lesbian, something Josie cannot really accept: **'I just want him to remember how he loved me. I want him to know I'm still his little girl.'**

Jim – he is the local fat-bellied Garda Sergeant. He notes that Ireland is now changed forever: **'There was a time when killing was for good, for God and country. That time is long gone.'**

Frank – he is the father to Bobby, who hates what his son has grown up to be. He lived through an abusive childhood, with a father who tried to beat the 'pride' out of him, and who is dead for one month when he tells his story from beyond the grave: **'I hadn't time to know I was dying before I was dead. I went quare easy in the end.'**

Triona – she is Bobby's wife and tries to provide an explanation for why Bobby and others behave as they do. She pledges her loyalty to Bobby throughout and is described by Bobby in glowing terms in his chapter: **'What matters only love?'**

Themes

1) Family

Family in General

Running through *The Spinning Heart* is a continuous reflection upon the family unit and how the **breakdown of society can be tied to the breakdown of the family**. The author does not provide any **commentary or judgement** on the theme, instead allowing each of the characters to speak for themselves and their own situation.

Selling the Family Land

The start of it all was the shooting dead of the young Cunliffe boy a number of years before, a boy who 'never threw a shape nor said a cross word', according to Bobby. His aunt then sold off the land.

Nothing good in *The Spinning Heart* comes from this decision by the aunt, as Pokey Burke's father, Josie, admits in hindsight: 'We should have known it would all end in tears. Around here, it all started with tears.' The division of the land, like 'our Lord's purple robe', thus removing the Cunliffe 'family name,' serves as a curse on the village, sending many people's hearts 'spinning' and their worlds toppling.

Incidentally, the fact that Josie loved one son (Eamonn) more than the other partly accounts for why Pokey turns out to be such a corrupt, selfish individual in adulthood. Josie admits all of this in his reflections.

Broken and Dysfunctional Families

The family circumstances described throughout are **almost all negative**. We discover that many of the characters have come from broken and dysfunctional families. Lloyd puts it bluntly: **'My Dad fucked off when I was a kid. I think he just couldn't stand to look at her anymore.'** This situation is mirrored in the lives of others:

- **Seanie** (father of Realtin's child, but distant)
- **Jason** (he is barred from even seeing his own child)
- **Denis** (his wife Kate can't stand the smell of him, among other things)
- **Lily** (her dearest son John refuses to speak to her, breaking her heart even more)
- **Trevor** (his schizophrenia may well be hereditary, or so he believes)
- **Josie** (he cannot accept Mags, who remains distant to him, because she is a lesbian)
- **Bobby** (he seems desperate for his marriage to Triona to work but he is deluding himself so long as he maintains an affair with Realtin)

There are examples of the breakdown of the family unit in every chapter. When taken together, *The Spinning Heart* portrays a world in which such breakdown is tied to the breakdown of wider society, leaving victims and broken people all around this rural village.

2) Suffering

Violence Brings Suffering

Frank Mahon is dead for a month when he voices his own story, the second-last chapter of the book. His **partly-comic, partly-tragic reflection is one of the most important in the book.** His soul is stuck as a 'ghost' in the spot where Denis, a local businessman who suffers a complete meltdown, chose to murder him with a plank of wood in a fury one evening. He experienced a painful and brutal death.

Suffering Continues

But the suffering has not yet ended. He is stuck in the same place, now that the Vatican 'got rid of purgatory.' He suffered at the hands of his own cruel father years before, who shouted, '**You know notten!**' at him the day he came home from school with great pride in himself. He now asks a question central to the fate of many characters in the novel:

> '**I wonder is this meant to be a punishment, to be confined to this cottage where I lived my whole life and where my father lived before me.**'

He poses this question on behalf of many who find themselves in situations they desperately want to escape from. In *The Spinning Heart*, despite the prosperity that the Celtic Tiger brought, **the characters now find themselves suffering the consequences of being stuck in a world they didn't really ask for or perhaps expect.**

Other Types of Suffering

- Realtin is in a situation that is strangely similar to Frank's, actually living in a 'ghost estate', with just one other neighbour, desperate to escape or avoid the **misery of living this way**, and longing to jump into bed with Bobby Mahon at any cost.
- The young male characters such as Rory and Brian suffer **disconnection** – neither of them can manage stable relationships with young women. Seanie Shaper, for all his shape-throwing and womanising, is suffering in the depths of utter despair and considers suicide.
- Trevor, the supposedly ugly and fat Montessori teacher, suffers from **acute pains and illnesses**, so much so that he considers kidnapping a child and 'saving' Realtin so as to overcome these personal problems.
- Timmy is **badly beaten** by Mickey Briars and regularly teased.
- Vasya is treated like so many migrant workers and suffers **embarrassment and indignity** that his proud heritage would not stand for.
- Bridie **weeps for her long-dead son.**
- Lloyd takes the bizarre position that he **exists in a universe of one** – a 'solipsist' – which is the ultimate escape mechanism from a world of suffering.
- To top it all, the **distance** that exists between Frank and Bobby, father and son, represents the gap that people all through the novel experience between their hopes and their failings. **The failure of people to overcome these gaps is what causes so**

much suffering. The final insult to Bobby is seen when he manages to frame himself for a murder he did not commit, much to the derision of the dead father, Frank: **'He hasn't a dust of sense.'**

Conclusion

Suffering is a key theme in *The Spinning Heart*, played out against a backdrop of everyday life, where what happens behind closed doors and in the minds of individual people can be a lot different to what we see on the surface.

Look carefully at how the writing skills in Paper 1 are then applied to 30-mark questions in Paper 2. Look at the example below.

 SAMPLE QUESTION AND ANSWER (30 MARKS/25 MINUTES)

The Spinning Heart by Donal Ryan (2018/19)

Question

Imagine that you are a resident of the town where the novel is set. Write a letter to Pokey Burke explaining how his actions have affected the community. Share your thoughts and feelings and indicate your knowledge of the text in doing so.

SAMPLE ANSWER:

Dear Pokey,

My name is Andrew Byrne and I am writing to you today to make you aware of the situation that your dishonesty and self-centred state of mind has caused in your home town.

You have left your litter all over the village. This is an eye-sore to the locality and is persuading new industries not to set up here which means there are no new jobs. It was bad enough that you failed to keep your own business afloat but you have left the town in a terrible mess also.

I was talking to Bobby Mahon lately, he is a sound lad. He told me that you did not give your employees their well-deserved stamps. He also cannot provide for his own family as he has no other work and doesn't qualify for social welfare.

Your disappearance off the scene has left this once peaceful place in turmoil. Your complete disregard for others has meant that people have lost hope. Since your act of cowardice, there has been a child kidnapped, a murder, and lots of family break-ups. These things may not all be your fault but at least when people were working they were happy and were living good lives together.

I hope that where you are now was worth all the pain and suffering that you caused. When you finish reading this letter, ask yourself one question: can you live with yourself?

I am hoping that this letter reaches you wherever you are now. I am hoping that it might spark some feelings of remorse. I am looking forward to seeing you back home some day so that face to face I can tell you that you are nothing but a spineless coward and a weasel.

Yours faithfully,

Andrew

(294 words)

EXAMINER'S ASSESSMENT

The candidate **completes the task** and makes a series of points directed at Pokey, although they seem a bit **disjointed**. The first reference to litter is **interesting** although it is not mentioned in the book. The vocabulary and expression is of a very good standard (afloat, turmoil, remorse, spineless, weasel). Sentences are well-crafted. Although **short**, it is a good effort, but below top standard.

MARKS AWARDED

7 + 6 + 7 + 3 = 23/30 (O3 Grade)

2. *The Great Gatsby* by F. Scott Fitzgerald (2018/19)

Storyline

- *The Great Gatsby* presents us with a straightforward but difficult dilemma*: **a handsome, wealthy young man is in love with a beautiful, young married woman.** We learn about the entire drama through the words of a narrator named Nick Carraway.

- Carraway, a young man from Minnesota, moves to New York in the summer of 1922. He rents a house in the West Egg district of Long Island, an unfashionable area populated by the 'new rich'. The mysterious Jay Gatsby lives in a **gigantic and gaudy*** mansion next door and throws extravagant parties every Saturday night.

- Nick drives out to the more 'old money' district of East Egg one evening for dinner with his cousin, Daisy Buchanan, and her husband, Tom. Daisy and Tom introduce

Nick to Jordan Baker, a beautiful but dishonest young woman who is a professional golfer. Nick begins an on-off romantic relationship with her.

- Jordan tells Nick that Tom also has a lover, Myrtle Wilson, who lives in the 'Valley of Ashes', a grey industrial dumping ground between West Egg and New York City. Not long after this, Nick travels to New York City with Tom and Myrtle. At a **vulgar,*** drunken party in the apartment that Tom keeps for their affair, Myrtle begins to **taunt*** Tom about Daisy, and Tom responds by breaking her nose.

WHO LIVES WHERE?		
West Egg	**East Egg**	**Valley of Ashes**
• Nick Carraway	• Tom Buchanan	• George Wilson
• Jay Gatsby	• Daisy Buchanan	• Myrtle Wilson
+	+	+
• Servants	• Jordan Baker visits regularly	• Small business owners like Michaelis and many thousands of low-paid workers
• Gardeners	• The 'old money' families who have been long established	
• The 'new money' residents whose houses are 'less fashionable' with 'wide lawns and friendly trees'		• The 'dumping ground' of society, halfway between the lights of the city and luxury of Long Island
Tom: 'Everyone in West Egg's a bootlegger' (Chapter 7)	Tom: 'I'd be a goddamn fool to live anywhere else' (Chapter 1)	Nick: 'the ash-grey men swarm up with leaden spades and stir up an impenetrable cloud, which screens their obscure operations from your sight' (Chapter 2)

- As the summer progresses, Nick eventually receives an invitation to one of Gatsby's legendary parties and meets Gatsby himself. He is a surprisingly young man who puts on an English accent, has a remarkable smile, and calls everyone 'old sport'. Gatsby is deeply in love with Daisy. He spends many nights staring at the green light at the end of her dock, across the bay from his mansion. Gatsby's extravagant lifestyle and wild parties are simply an attempt to impress Daisy. Gatsby wants Nick to arrange a reunion between himself and Daisy. After an initially awkward meeting in Nick's house, Gatsby and Daisy feel their love is reawakened, so they begin an affair.

- Tom grows increasingly suspicious of his wife's relationship with Gatsby and eventually realises that Gatsby is in love with her. He forces the group to drive into New York City, where he confronts Gatsby in a suite at the Plaza Hotel. Tom claims that he and Daisy have a history that Gatsby could never understand. He also announces that Gatsby is a criminal – his fortune comes from **bootlegging*** alcohol and other illegal activities. Daisy realises that her true commitment is to Tom, not Gatsby. To prove his assertiveness, and to get the upper hand on Gatsby,

Tom insists that Gatsby and Daisy drive back home to Long Island together, while the others will follow behind.

- When Nick, Jordan and Tom drive through the Valley of Ashes, however, they discover that Gatsby's car has struck and killed Myrtle, Tom's lover. Nick learns that Daisy was driving the car when it struck Myrtle, but that Gatsby intends to take the blame. The next day, Tom tells Myrtle's husband, George, that Gatsby was the driver of the car. George, who has leapt to the conclusion that the driver of the car that killed Myrtle must have been her lover, finds Gatsby in the swimming pool at his mansion and shoots him dead. He then fatally shoots himself.

- Nick stages a small funeral for Gatsby. Hardly anybody attends, though his father comes from North Dakota for the burial of his boy 'Jimmy'. 'Owl-Eyes' also turns up, and it is suggested that he really has no life of his own apart from his fascination with Gatsby. Nick ends his relationship with Jordan, and moves back to the Midwest. The Buchanans 'disappear' for the time being. Nick reflects that the era of dreaming – both Gatsby's dream and the American dream – is over.

Five Key Words

- **Dilemma** – difficult situation, problem, obstacle
- **Gaudy** – tasteless, flashy, lacking real style, cheap
- **Vulgar** – crude, common, low-quality
- **Taunt** – to tease, to annoy, to provoke
- **Bootlegging** – illegal trading of goods

CHARACTERS

The characters to concentrate on when revising are:

- Jay Gatsby
- Daisy Buchanan
- Tom Buchanan
- Jordan Baker
- Nick Carraway

George Wilson and **Myrtle Wilson** as well as **Meyer Wolfsheim** are significant characters, but mostly as part of the unfolding plot. The majority of the action and the significant themes of the novel concern the five above.

1) Jay Gatsby – the 'protagonist' of the novel

- His great desire is to be reunited with Daisy Buchanan, the love he lost five years earlier. His quest for her heart mirrors the quest for the so-called 'American Dream' of unlimited success and achievement.

- Gatsby, whose real name is Jay Gatz, is initially a **mysterious figure,** considered 'great' in that he is fabulously wealthy, warm-hearted and generous. He has a decorated military record also ('"Major Jay Gatsby," I read, "For extraordinary Valour"'.)

- But all great heroes have a fatal flaw: **Gatsby's flaw is that he cannot separate his dream from reality.** His pursuit of Daisy, with his lavish parties and showings of wealth, cannot overcome the fact that her true allegiance, as a married woman of the middle classes, is to her husband, Tom.

- He is a **romantic idealist:** there is a sense that **Gatsby loves the idea of Daisy rather than the reality of a loving, lasting relationship.** This is memorably shown at the end of Chapter 7. Gatsby is standing guard outside of Daisy's house on a pathetic vigil. He is completely unable to realise that **his dream is not a reality** and so stands watching for a sign from Daisy.

- We discover from **Meyer Wolfsheim** that Gatsby's fortune is derived from criminality ('bootlegging').

- Very few people turn up to his funeral, signifying how alone he ultimately was and how shallow his pursuit of the 'dream' really was.

2) Daisy Buchanan – what we would consider a 'trophy bride' today

- She is undoubtedly **beautiful** and **captivating,** with a sultry voice, and represents women of the elite social classes. Her privileged upbringing in Louisville created **expectations of a particular lifestyle,** which Tom, her husband, is able to provide.

- She is the object of Gatsby's dreams. She has a **continuous tendency to appear weak and frail,** as if she needs to be rescued from herself or something else.

- Her first words are spoken to Nick, who is her cousin, who drops by for a visit: *'I'm p-paralysed with happiness.'* It is an early suggestion of the **contradictions that exist in the lives of the main characters.** Daisy is somewhere between being paralysed and being happy.

- Shortly afterwards, Daisy admits to Nick that she is now **'pretty cynical about everything',** as a consequence of her life choices. Most telling of all is Daisy's famous remark upon realising that she has given birth to a baby girl, who is named Pammy: *'And I hope she'll be a fool – that's the best thing a girl can be in this world, a beautiful little fool.'* This contrast between perception and reality is seen in the life of Daisy Buchanan.

3) Tom Buchanan – Daisy's husband, an upper-class alpha male

- Tom Buchanan comes from an old, wealthy, Chicago family and takes pride in his rough obnoxious and forceful demeanour. He is very used to being in control, with questionable morals. He is **unashamedly racist** at a time when such attitudes were encouraged: *'It's up to us, who are the dominant race, to watch out or these other races will have control of things.'*

- He is an important character in that he provides a **strong contrast** to the more thoughtful and reflective character of Gatsby and also Nick, who exhibit more mannerly behaviours in public.
- He carries on an adulterous affair with Myrtle, for whom he has **little or no respect**. Nick tells us in Chapter 2 of his violent side: *'Making a short deft movement, Tom Buchanan broke her nose with his open hand.'*
- His involvement in the plot concludes following the car crash on the way back from New York. He reassures Daisy that all will be fine as they sit together in their house, with the **pathetic Gatsby looking in the window.**
- The next day, they leave and are never heard from again, except when Nick spots him in Manhattan the following October.

4) Jordan Baker – a friend of Daisy and a sometime lover of Nick

- She is a female professional golfer with a **questionable reputation**. There is a suggestion that she cheated to win a tournament.
- Her **assertive and competitive nature** contrasts with the helplessness and weakness of Daisy.
- She comes across as somewhat **shallow** in her approach to life, seen in her attitude to driving and causing crashes: *'"They'll keep out of my way" she insisted. "It takes two to make an accident."'*
- Nick observes that in fact she is **'incurably dishonest'** and had been **'dealing in subterfuges'** for much of her life. She meets Nick again near the end of the novel, by which time she is engaged to another man. They depart on relatively good terms.
- He prefers to call their relationship **'a tender curiosity'**.

5) Nick Carraway – the story's narrator

- Nick rents the small house next to Gatsby's mansion in West Egg and over the course of events helps Gatsby to reunite with Daisy, a reunion that takes place in Nick's house.
- He is one of the most famous and studied narrative 'voices' in the modern novel format. He is **caught between being a detached observer of the unfolding drama around him and being part of the same drama.**
- In the aftermath of Gatsby's death, it is Nick who effectively becomes the sole accomplice of Gatsby, handling all of the funeral and legal affairs: *'I found myself on Gatsby's side, and alone. From the moment I telephoned news of the catastrophe to West Egg Village, every surmise about him, and every practical question, was referred to me.'*
- One really important point about Nick is that while the novel is called *The Great Gatsby*, **it is really Nick Carraway's version of events**. The narrator therefore is very like the reader or student, pondering what to make of people like the Buchanans and the Gatsbys of the world.

- We are never entirely sure, but students can conclude that **Nick Carraway is glad to have the whole episode behind him** when he writes his story.

Other Characters

- **Myrtle and George Wilson:**
  - **Representative of the lower or 'working' class**
  - They appear **trapped** by their position in society
  - Stuck in the **symbolic** 'Valley of Ashes'
  - They express the **desperation of many people at this time**, wishing for a better life
  - Myrtle is **killed violently** by Daisy, who runs her over
  - George, a **'God-fearing man'**, ends up killing Gatsby
- **Meyer Wolfshiem:**
  - Gatsby's business associate and **link to organised crime**
  - He is **completely untrustworthy** and typical of the **type of people Gatsby had dealings with**
  - He makes perhaps the most **ironic** and **hypocritical** statement of the novel, when he meets Nick: **'Yeah Gatsby's real careful about women. He would never so much as look at a friend's wife.'**
  - He fails to turn up at the funeral despite all he has been through with Gatsby

Themes

1) Dreams Versus Reality

- *The Great Gatsby* considers the **'American Dream'** and what happens to people when the **dream does not work out.**
- Nick, reflecting on Gatsby's death, observes at the very end that **'he had come a long way to this blue lawn and his dream must have seemed so close that he could hardly fail to grasp it.'** He is to be admired for following his dream.
- Ultimately **Gatsby cannot buy Daisy's love.** He dreams of a life everlasting with her but he also believes that he can control the emotions and decisions of people at his will, most effectively because he is now wealthy. That is not the reality of the world.
- **Gatsby loves the idea of loving Daisy** but cannot make it happen no matter what Nick or Jordan or anybody else says or does.

The novel is full of other characters who, for one reason or another, are immersed in their own dreams as they avoid the reality around them:

- The 1920s saw an increase in greed, indulgence and careless living. The partygoers at Gatsby's mansion (Chapter 3) indulge in **drunken debauchery** amid a scene of **fake friendliness.**

- Many people don't even know who everybody else is and **nobody seems to care.** Afterwards, *'eight servants, including an extra gardener, toiled all day with mops and garden-shears, repairing the ravages of the night before.'*
- Myrtle Wilson engages in an affair with Tom Buchanan. She confides to Nick about her first time with Tom and she finishes her story with the words: *'You can't live forever.'*
- Minor characters like the 'boarder' named Klipspringer and an older gentleman referred to as 'Owl-Eyes' hang around Gatsby's mansion as if they have **no life of their own.** Both could be classed as 'odd' individuals who seem in **search of some connection with people** in the real world. Neither appear to have any real friends.

2) Social Class

The two localities of East and West Egg symbolise the **difference between the old and the new in 1920s America.** The new-rich of West Egg **threaten the social order and the status of people like Tom and Daisy.**

- The old values of hard work, honesty and determination is seen in traditional middle-class families like the Buchanans from Chicago and the Fays from Kentucky.
- This is why Jay Gatsby is so despised by Tom Buchanan, never mind the fact that he desires his wife. Tom dismisses him at every opportunity: *'All this "old sport" business. Where'd you pick that up?'*
- Furthermore, those who attend Gatsby's parties are themselves competing with each other to **climb the social ladder,** to somehow earn respectability in an increasingly competitive post-war America.
- We graphically see the class divide in both the Valley of Ashes and in Manhattan. George Wilson is an honest, hard-working man who is exploited on a number of levels by the wealthy Tom: *'He's so dumb he doesn't know he is alive.'*
- A grey old man makes money selling half-bred puppy dogs. Again Tom gives him money and tells him *'go buy ten more dogs with it.'* The **condescension** and **arrogance** of Tom speaks of the social class divide that he was determined to preserve.

exam focus

Look carefully at how the writing skills in Paper 1 are then applied to 30-mark questions in Paper 2. Look at the example on the next page.

SAMPLE QUESTION AND ANSWER (30 MARKS/25 MINUTES)

The Great Gatsby by F. Scott Fitzgerald (2018/19)

Question

Imagine that you are a newspaper reporter. Following the death of Jay Gatsby, write an article about his exciting life and violent death. Your article should demonstrate your knowledge of the novel, *The Great Gatsby*.

SAMPLE ANSWER:

The *New York Inquirer* Special Report

'LEGACY OF LEGENDARY WEST EGG RESIDENT'

Questions remain unanswered nearly a month after the death of one of the nation's most infamous celebrity party hosts. Jay Gatsby was found dead in his own swimming pool, having been shot at close range a number of times on September 2nd. George Wilson from the nearby Valley of Ashes was named as being responsible, who then went on to kill himself shortly afterwards. But the exact motive behind Wilson's actions has puzzled many observers. There are claims that Gatsby may have had some hand to play in the accidental death of Wilson's wife Myrtle at this time, however eyewitness accounts seem to contradict each other. The absence of any clear evidence means this case will continue to interest commentators for some time over here.

So what did Gatsby do to get himself killed, and more importantly, who exactly was he? He first came to the attention of New York residents when he started hosting lavish parties out on Long Island. Everybody who was anybody seemed to turn up uninvited to night-long celebrations that seemed to happen for no particular reason. He had a huge staff employed at each party, including a waiter whose only job was to press a button to make fresh orange juice on the spot. With America on the wave of success, nobody seemed to care much about why they were there, who anybody was and what exactly they were doing. They simply had a great time. Actresses, singers, producers, Wall Street executives, bankers, book publishers, sport stars and many others flocked to his house to be entertained by full orchestras for hours on end. He had connections to the sporting world via professional golfer Jordan Baker, while his association with the family of Mr and Mrs Tom Buchanan was also noted. Further back, he graduated from Oxford University, saw action in the War and was decorated by the military for his efforts.

Gatsby was a curious man: he usually stood away from everybody else, smiled at everybody as they came and went, and nobody really knew much of who he was. He spoke with a slight hint of an English accent. Very few really got to speak to him intimately. His closest neighbour, Nick Carraway, has been reluctant to say much about him since the death. The only comment he made when questioned by our reporters was that Gatsby 'liked to live the dream; one day, his dream ended. That's about it.' This reluctance to talk has made many people wonder about the source of Gatsby's apparent wealth. He was in the 'bond business' like many of his age. He was also seen on occasion in Manhattan with the well-known Jewish businessman Meyer Wolfsheim. But what was most unusual was the absence of friends and family at his funeral, which was arranged and paid for by Carraway. The deceased's father, a 'Mr Gatz' from North Dakota, did appear. He was a man who did not seem to benefit from his son's great wealth, appearing as a frail and quite poorly dressed individual. It is surprising that no other relatives turned up, nor did anybody seem to grieve for his passing, except for Mr Gatz himself. These circumstances are certainly strange. The ongoing reluctance for people to speak about his life and death can only lead us to conclude that there was a lot more to Mr Jay Gatsby than the party nights would have shown.

(570 words)

EXAMINER'S ASSESSMENT

Excellent register here; very much like a piece from a newspaper. A lot of **detail** is covered and **knowledge of the story** is evident. Clever use of an imaginary **quotation** shows a high level of **engagement**. Excellent vocabulary – sentences are very well constructed. A top-class effort at this task.

MARKS AWARDED

9 + 9 + 9 + 3 = 30/30 (O1 Grade)

3. *The Plough and the Stars* by Sean O'Casey (2018)

Storyline

ACT 1 – The play begins in **November 1915**, set in a **tenement*** building in Dublin City.

- **Fluther Good**, a carpenter and drunkard, is repairing a door to the Clitheroe flat while gossiping with **Mrs Gogan**, a neighbour who has a new baby and a dying teenage daughter, **Mollser**.
- A meeting of the Irish Citizen Army, the Irish Volunteers and the Irish National Foresters is to be held that night. These groups form the basis of the rebel army of the **1916 Rising**.
- **Jack Clitheroe**, husband of **Nora**, is caught up in the **revolutionary*** movement. But Nora wants to build a respectable home for them both. **This is the main point of conflict between the newly married couple:** Jack is committed to Irish freedom but Nora is committed to building a stable, happy home life.
- Jack is also disliked by the protestant **Bessie Burgess**, who lives on the top floor and who is also fond of a drink and singing the praises of the British Crown. She also has a son fighting the front line in the Second World War.
- Nora's uncle **Peter** and another character, **Young Covey**, who is Jack's cousin, involve themselves in discussing politics. These two characters share the flat with the Clitheroes.
- Jack is promoted to commandant, via a message from a **Captain Brennan**, a 'chicken-butcher' of the Irish Citizen Army. Jack leaves to attend a gathering that night.

ACT 2 – We enter a 'commodious public house' where we meet the prostitute **Rosie Redmond**. Outside, the meeting is being held and the audience regularly hears the 'voice at the window' call for bloody revolution.

- Rosie complains that the meeting is bad for business, even though Peter, Fluther and to a lesser extent, the Covey, are impressed by the powerful speeches.
- Various other characters enter. What follows is a series of **tragi-comic*** arguments, amid lots of drinking and shouting, mostly about the Irish fight for freedom, as the bartender tries to keep order.
- This brilliant scene concludes after Jack arrives with **Captain Brennan** and a **Lieutenant Langon** from the Irish Volunteers. They proudly display both the Plough and the Stars (the banner of the ICA) and the Irish tricolour. They drink together, vowing to die for Ireland.
- They storm back out to the rally, and Fluther stumbles homeward with Rosie.

ACT 3 – We skip forward to Easter Week 1916.

- At the start of Act 3, the Rising is underway, Fluther and Nora are missing, Mollser is **terminally*** ill and characters gather outside the tenement.

- Nora arrives back with Fluther; they have been searching for Jack. Nora is pregnant and in a state of great distress.
- Bessie Burgess shouts from the top of the tenement in support of the now booming British artillery guns. Bessie, Mrs Gogan and later Fluther head off to do some looting themselves, returning near the end of the scene with all kinds of stolen goods.
- Meanwhile, Jack and Captain Brennan enter with a badly wounded Lieutenant Langon.
- Nora becomes even more distressed with the scene, while Mollser is in her last moments. A doctor is badly needed, and since Fluther is too drunk to do anything, it is Bessie Burgess who heads out into the gunfire to seek help.

ACT 4 – A few days later, when the action switches upstairs to Bessie Burgess's dingy tenement room.

- Mollser's coffin is in the room. Nora has had a miscarriage and a nervous breakdown.
- Peter, the Covey and Fluther play cards upon the coffin as they keep watch out the window. Captain Brennan arrives to announce that Jack is also dead. Brennan needs to seek refuge in the tenement so he removes his army uniform.

- Two British soldiers, Stoddart and Tinley, arrive to search the house and to take out the coffin for burial. They also announce that all men are to be rounded up, as they are seeking a sniper in the area.
- In the confusion that erupts, Bessie Burgess is accidently shot as she tries to keep Nora from screaming out the window in **anguish***. Bessie dies slowly and painfully while Nora tries to make tea.
- Mrs Gogan manages to take Nora away and hold her together. The two British soldiers return, convinced that they have shot the sniper until they see that they have accidentally killed Bessie.
- As the shelling outside intensifies with the assault on the rebels' stronghold in the GPO, the soldiers sing a British Army tune. This concludes the play, suggesting the failure of the 1916 Rising, an idea that O'Casey strongly hinted at in this play.

Five Key Words

- **Tenement** – a usually overcrowded, poor-quality city apartment
- **Revolutionary** – a state of uprising against the government
- **Tragi-comic** – a mixture of humour and sadness
- **Terminally** – at the end, the conclusion, no way out
- **Anguish** – great pain, mental suffering

Some important notes on revising *The Plough and the Stars*

- A knowledge of the main incidents and the main groups involved in the **1916 Rising** would be helpful in revising.
- This text is a **drama, written to be experienced on stage in a theatre.** If you don't get to see a live performance, it is very useful to watch a DVD version, or watch some scenes on YouTube if possible.
- O'Casey also chose to include a very strong Dublin working-class dialect in his writing. An **audio version of the text** will make it much easier to understand.
- O'Casey does not present a straightforward story with one plot and with one scene following another. Instead, he prefers to run a **series of story-lines side-by-side,** which is a bit like a soap opera today. So studying important characters (see below) is very valuable.
- **Act 2 is a little play in itself.** It captures many of the themes and ideas that O'Casey wanted to emphasise in the play: politics, poverty, family life, suffering, sacrifice. Read this act closely when revising.

CHARACTERS

There are sixteen characters in the play.

- Eight of them live together in the tenement:
  Jack, Nora, Peter, the Covey, Fluther, Bessie, Mrs Gogan, Mollser
- Four others are in the army: two Irish and two British
  Irish = Captain Brennan, Lieutenant Langon
  British = Corporal Stoddart, Sergeant Tinley
- One is a prostitute – Rosie Redmond
- One is a bartender – he says very little
- One is a 'Woman from Rathmines' who is lost
- One is the 'Voice at the window', which is meant to be Padraig Pearse.

Of the eight tenement residents, four are most interesting for revision purposes:

- **Nora – especially her relationship with Jack**
- **Bessie**
- **Fluther**
- **The Young Covey**

1) Nora Clitheroe

A young Dublin woman, recently married to **Jack**, a bricklayer and commandant in the Irish Citizen Army.

- She seeks **respectability** and is determined to get out of the tenements to a new life.
- She **attempts to bring order** to the chaotic tenement.
- She scolds Peter and the Covey in Act 1: *'Are yous always goin' to be tearin' down the little bit of respectability that a body's thryin' to build up?'*
- She **symbolises the ideals of marriage, happiness and traditional family values**.
- She loses both her husband, to war, and her unborn child, to miscarriage.
- It confirms for us that **the play is a tragedy at the personal level,** best seen in Nora's fate.

2) Fluther Good

Drinks too much and is unreliable at times, but he represents the many thousands of ordinary working-class men living amid great poverty in Dublin at the time.

- He drinks to forget about the squalor of daily life. He is a **realistic depiction of the comical working-class Dubliner**, who also displays a sense of **decency** and **friendliness**.
- He is caught up in the fervour of the Rising in Act 2, but Fluther and many like him **care little for the rebellion**. They are pressed by the need for more basic things like food, shelter and contentment.
- He comes home from a looting spree in Act 3, delighted with his exploits, shouting, *'Th' whole city can topple home to hell, for Fluther!'*
- We cannot totally admire Fluther, as **he fails Nora in her greatest hour of need** at the end of the play, being blind drunk again.
- He symbolises many of the men of the time who seem **incapable of managing daily life** and therefore not capable of building a new independent and free Ireland.

3) Bessie Burgess

A Protestant, loyal to the British throne, which makes her an **outsider** in the tenement.

- She is a widow with a son fighting the Germans on the front line in the First World War. She proudly displays the British flag during the rising and sings 'Rule Britannia' from her top window.
- She has a clear conscience in everything she does: *'If you think, me lassie, that Bessie Burgess has an untidy conscience, she'll soon show you th' differ!'*
- O'Casey presents her as being both **hostile and generous, aggressive but also tender and caring**.

- She invokes God regularly in times of need, such as at the end of Act 3 when she bravely goes in search of a doctor for Nora: *'Oh God, be thou my help in time o' throuble. An' shelter me safely in th' shadow of Thy wings!'*

- Her compassion, care and maternal strength show a **likeable side** to her character. This is seen especially in her valiant attempts to help Nora, Mollser and Mrs Gogan, even though she regularly fights with them in the tenement.

- Her accidental death heightens the sense of tragedy. It is cruel that **the one real defender of the British presence is then shot by the very soldiers she is praising.**

4) The Young Covey

The character who voices the **opinions of O'Casey himself** in the play.

- He is something of an intellectual, self-taught and who has read important writings on politics.

- O'Casey uses the character of the Covey to speak his view that the **1916 Rising essentially failed the working people of Ireland.** This is best summed up by the Covey as he chats to the prostitute Rosie in Act 2: *'What's the use of freedom if it's not economic freedom?'* to which Rosie replies in agreement, given her lack of business that night.

- But his role is important in that he **balances out the idealism of the Irish Volunteers.**

- In the final act, while speaking to the British soldiers, he states that *'the only duty of a socialist is the emancipation of the workers.'*

- The ramblings and arguments of the Young Covey are an important feature of the play, as they reflect the **political opinions of O'Casey** and the **reasons why the Rising is shown to be a failure.**

Other Characters

There is no 'main character' as such in the play. O'Casey did not write it in that way. There are some points we can note, however:

- The men, particularly the Irish Volunteers, are presented as **weak and ineffective.**
  - They are listed as a bricklayer, a Civil Servant and a 'chicken-butcher', hardly the sort to defeat the might of the British Empire.
  - They appear caught up in a **sense of romantic fanaticism** as they have no real hope of winning any real war.
  - They are inspired by the 'Voice at the Window' calling for sacrifice, bloodshed and a welcome for war as an 'Angel of God'.
  - When the reality of the British soldiers arrives, they are no match.

- On the other hand, the female characters are shown to be far more **resilient, determined and admirable.**
  - Mrs Gogan is a feisty woman who is nursing a new baby and a dying teenage daughter. She does whatever she can to support them in their need, including looting.
  - Nora, Bessie and Rosie are all well capable of standing up for themselves in the face of very difficult circumstances.
  - In general, the women are presented in a sympathetic way by O'Casey, despite their flaws and weaknesses.
- The two British soldiers, Stoddart and Tinley, are both presented as **men just doing their job.**
  - They are surprisingly polite and conversational when they appear in the tenement in Act 4, although they maintain an air of authority and menace.
  - In shooting Bessie Burgess, they show no remorse or regret. This shows that death and killing was commonplace at the time and that life such as this was considered cheap: *'Oh, dead as bedamned. Well, we couldn't afford to toike any chawnces.'*
  - The play concludes with the two soldiers singing an army tune as if they have scored a 'victory' of sorts.

Themes

1) Politics

Sean O'Casey viewed the **1916 Rising as a failure**. This is the most important theme in the play.

Misguided Freedom Fighters

- It was a failure because it failed the ordinary working-class people, who were very much the majority in Ireland at the time. **Nobody in the tenement benefitted** at all from the events of 1916.
- The Covey articulates O'Casey's view most closely. He notes that there is a 'disgrace' being brought to the banner of the labour movement (The 'plough and the stars') and that it should only be used to build a 'workers republic', or a **country that benefitted the working-class people the most**.
- Uncle Peter is a weak-minded Irish nationalist who simply **hopes** for freedom. But he is fairly **ineffective** in bringing it about. He is part of the 'Irish Foresters' who

seem more interested in commemorating the death of Wolfe Tone in 1798 than actually fighting for real.

- Fluther is clearly a 'Public-House Nationalist' who is most excited about the fate of Ireland **when he is full of drink**. In reality, he does not take arms at all nor make any significant contribution to the rebellion in any way.

Jack Clitheroe – the most misguided of all?

- **Jack Clitheroe** is the character whose political motivations can be most severely criticised.
- Motivated by the blood-filled, high-minded speeches of 'the voice at the window' (Padraig Pearse), **Jack deserts his wife Nora** and says that *'Ireland is greater than a wife'.* He rushes headlong into battle with little thought of consequence, **motivated by a kind of 'vanity'**.
- He gets to wear a uniform, he gets to command others and ultimately he gets to die heroically for Ireland. In O'Casey's mind, this was **an utter waste of life** and brought nothing but misery to those affected.
- The politics of Bessie Burgess acts as a counter-balance to all this nationalism. It is **truly tragic** that she is the one who ends up dying in her own home, on stage, shot by the very people she had been defending politically throughout the play.

2) 'Notions of Upperosity'

There is a great line in the play spoken by Mrs Gogan right at the start of the action. A new hat is delivered to the tenement for Nora, and Mrs Gogan takes it out of the box: *'That hat now, cost more than a penny. Such notions of upperosity she's gettin'.'* This demonstrates the brilliant wit and colour of the Dublin dialect as well as O'Casey's skill as a playwright. He introduces us to a powerful theme of the play, which is how people of this time tried to better themselves in the lower social classes.

Nora's 'Notions'

Nora symbolises a desire for respectability and a brighter future for herself and Jack, to rise above poverty and suffering. This is a **recurring theme** in the play. But this causes problems because characters who try to make something of themselves are usually ridiculed.

- Mrs Gogan is threatened by the idea of Nora rising above the ordinary and making something of herself as it will mean she is now 'above' her socially. Her **'upperosity' is not welcome in the tenements**.
- The Covey is continually taunted in spite of his **attempts to educate himself**. His knowledge of socialist literature is scorned by Fluther, along with his pronunciation of scholarly words such as 'mollycewells'.
- The paintings on the walls of Nora's flat are **considered indecent** or somewhat immoral.
- Bessie Burgess reminds us that **many a good person was reared in a tenement**, effectively saying there is no need to want to live elsewhere.

- Rosie **criticises the religious commitment of many Irish volunteers**, many of whom were motivated by a type of religious conviction to fight for a Catholic Ireland.
- The mysterious **'Woman from Rathmines'** appears in Act 3 and nobody wants to help her. She is a middle-class stereotype with whom **the characters have absolutely nothing in common**, even though they live just a few miles apart. It is as if this respectable, wealthy person is from another planet, one that the characters would not like to visit.

In conclusion, O'Casey presents a collection of characters who, on the one hand, desire a better life, but on the other, have grave suspicions of people who might develop 'notions' above their station. It is as if these characters are **destined to remain** in poverty as long as they keep up this attitude of not accepting any 'upperosity'.

exam focus

Your notes on characters and themes can help you answer the short 10-mark question on the day. Look at this example below.

exam Q

SAMPLE QUESTION AND ANSWER (10 MARKS/8 MINUTES)

The Plough and the Stars by Sean O'Casey (2018)

Question

Do you think that Jack was right to leave Nora and join Captain Brennan at the end of Act 1? Give one reason for your answer. (10)

SAMPLE ANSWER:

> I think that Jack Clithroe was foolish and very wrong to join Captain Brennan at the end of Act 1. The whole point of the play was to show how wrong the 1916 Rising was. Jack is the character who dies trying to fight the British. This is because he thought that 'Ireland is greater than a wife', so he leaves Nora even though she is pregnant and then goes off on easter Monday to try get irish freedom. He is wrong because he should have known that his wife needed him more than the army did and that we had no chance of beating them. So that is why i think he was wrong to join captain Brennan.
>
> (199 words)

EXAMINER'S ASSESSMENT

The question is addressed, there is a quote and some following comment. The vocabulary and expression is basic and there are some minor errors but overall this is a solid answer.

MARKS AWARDED

4 + 3 = 7/10 (O3 Grade)

4. *The Playboy of the Western World* by J. M. Synge (2019)

Storyline

The entire play is set in a pub 'on the wild coast of Mayo', some time around 1907. It has three acts.

ACT 1 – Pegeen Mike, daughter of the pub owner Michael James Flaherty, writes a list of essentials for her upcoming wedding. She is engaged to a local 'fat and fair young man' named Shawn Keogh.

- Her father and his drinking friends are attending a local wake and she makes arrangements for the wedding as Shawn looks on. Her father returns, and demands that Shawn stay overnight with Pegeen. He refuses, for fear the priest might not allow it.
- Shawn then tells of seeing a wild man in a ditch earlier that day. It turns out that this man is Christy Mahon, the young **'playboy'** of the story.
- Christy then enters the pub, quite dirty and appearing to be frightened. He tells an amazing story of being on the run, having killed his own father.
- The locals are initially very impressed by his story and he is offered a job by Michael right away.
- Pegeen instantly falls for his **charm*** and she dismisses the **cowardly** Shawn from the pub.
- The Widow Quin hears of the playboy's arrival and takes great interest, but again, Pegeen sends her off.
- Pegeen's upcoming marriage disappoints the playboy, who wonders to himself why he didn't kill his father sooner, if he had known such affection and attention would come his way. He sleeps soundly.

ACT 2 – The next day, the playboy's arrival causes much **upheaval*** and excitement in the village.

- He tells of how he murdered his father with a spade, as his father had demanded that he marry an ugly old widow. Local girls seek his affection, while Shawn **conspires*** with the Widow Quin to try to get him to leave, even offering him money and clothes.
- He finds himself entered in the local sports day on the beach later that afternoon. However, soon after, his father, 'Old Mahon' – bandaged, bloodied but still very much alive – arrives in the village.

- The Widow sends Old Mahon off to the harbour, while she decides to try to arrange a quick marriage between Christy and Pegeen. She hopes that she will receive **privileges*** in the pub from then onwards.

ACT 3 – Later that evening, news of the playboy's great feats in the local sports day are spoken of in the pub.

- Old Mahon returns once more and grows increasingly suspicious. Widow Quin convinces him that he is mad, given the bad head injury he has suffered. He leaves again, in search of Christy.
- While the crowds watch the final events on the beach, Christy proposes to Pegeen and she accepts. But her father Michael enters along with Shawn, and they insist that she must marry Shawn.
- Christy offers to fight Shawn for her, so when Shawn refuses to fight, her father changes his mind and agrees to her marriage to the playboy.
- However, Old Mahon returns once more and the truth about Christy emerges. He isn't nearly as brave and as wild as his story suggests.
- This leads to another fight between father and son and offstage we hear a loud cry and then silence. With this turn of events, the locals no longer approve of Christy so they attempt to tie him up and bring him to the police.

- Amid much violent struggling and arguing, Old Mahon crawls in yet again, this time demanding that Christy be released and promising that they both will leave Mayo forever.
- Christy refuses to leave peacefully and they both exit in serious discomfort.
- Shawn decides to remind Pegeen of her marriage arrangement with him. She boxes his ears and **laments*** that she has lost the only playboy of the western world. This is the closing line of the play.

Five Key Words
- **Charm** – pleasing, appealing personality
- **Upheaval** – a sense of chaos, disturbance, trouble
- **Conspire** – to plan secretly, illegally, to work together
- **Privilege** – a special benefit, advantage or exemption
- **Lament** – a cry of pain, sadness, loss or mourning

Some important notes on revising *The Playboy of the Western World*

- This text is a **drama, written to be experienced on stage in a theatre**. If you don't get to see a live performance, it is very useful to **watch a DVD version** or watch some scenes on YouTube if possible.
- The play is full of poetic phrases and heavily accented lines. (e.g. Christy describes his murderous act: **'I just riz the loy and let fall the edge of it on his skull.'**) This can make it a little difficult to read. However, an **audio version of the text** will make it much easier to understand.
- Synge chose to write this play based upon his experiences with people from the **Aran Islands** and other places in the West of Ireland.
- He was criticised heavily at the time by some Irish critics. Some felt that he was patronising and poking fun at the supposed **backwardness of Irish country people**, especially rural Catholics. Synge himself was a middle-class Protestant, born in Wicklow. He said that **the play was based on 'a true story'**.

CHARACTERS

There are twelve characters, plus some 'peasants' listed in the cast. The most complex characters are the ones to focus on:

- Christy Mahon
- Pegeen Mike
- the Widow Quin

These three characters provide us with many insights and important quotes from the play. The other characters (the 'girls' and the 'farmers', etc.) tend to provide background noise and observations, but not much that is very significant for revision.

1) Christy Mahon – playboy or chancer?

- He is the **handsome and charming 'playboy'**, aged in his twenties. He is on the run because he has murdered his father, Old Mahon.
- He **earns the affection of his hosts** rather quickly, especially Pegeen Mike, to whom he is then briefly engaged.
- The locals love his **rebellious spirit**. His life seems to be the **opposite of their dull, boring and predictable lives**.
- He is a **fine athlete** and demonstrates great skills at the local sports day, much to the local girls' enjoyment.
- He cannot believe his **luck** by the end of Act 1 to have *'two fine women fighting for the likes of me.'* He wonders why he didn't kill his father before now.
- He represents the **freedom and adventure that many of the local people would love to have**. However, Christy is nowhere near as brave and dashing as he makes himself out to be.

- Old Mahon calls Christy:

  'a dirty, stuttering lout'

  'a lier on walls, a talker of folly, a man you'd see stretched the half of the day in the brown ferns with his belly to the sun'

  'drunk on the smell of a pint'

- By the end, he has attempted to kill his father a total of three times, without success.
- Mike's attitude also changes towards him, calling him a *'lousy schemer' and a 'frisky rascal'.*
- He leaves in disgrace, dragging his father with him, but not before biting Shawn in the leg and cursing everybody around for the way things have worked out.

Conclusion

- He is far from heroic and more likely what we would call a **'chancer'** in today's language.

2) Pegeen Mike – the love interest

- She speaks one of the most important lines in the play: *'there's a great gap between a gallous story and a dirty deed.'* This summarises a central question of the play: is Christy Mahon a character to be admired or to be despised?
- Synge sets this question up via the notion of marriage. Would a **fine country girl**, daughter of a publican and businessman, truly want to marry such a man?
- Pegeen, aged in her twenties, is no doubt a **strong-willed and quick-thinking young woman**. She has a rebellious and independent streak, being quick to challenge Church authority, at least while standing in her own public house.
- She tells Shawn to *'stop tormenting me with Father Reilly'* and she wittily remarks that the Pope *'wouldn't bother with this place'.*
- She is well able to challenge Christy, the playboy, and doubts his story from the start: *'A soft lad the like of you wouldn't slit the windpipe of a screeching sow.'*
- For Pegeen Mike, she faces a future that is either a dull, loveless marriage to Shawn, or something more adventurous and exotic in an attachment to the playboy: *'Wouldn't it be a bitter thing for a girl to go marrying the like of Shawneen, and he a middling kind of scarecrow, with no savagery or fine words in him at all?'*
- When she then realises the lies that Christy has told, and when she sees the real 'savagery' of father and son brawling, she faces the reality that the playboy, the *'ugly liar, was playing off the hero, and the fright of men.'*

3) The Widow Quin – the 'older woman' and love rival?

- A woman of 'about thirty', her widowed status meant that she had considerable 'experience' in terms of life's hardships and realities.

- She acts as an **antagonist** in the play, causing mischief, trying to keep one step ahead of Pegeen and Christy and **manipulating others to her advantage**.
- She sees herself as a suitable wife for the playboy, having supposedly killed her own husband. She is the **'love rival'** initially once the playboy arrives.
- However, she sees that marriage is unlikely so she then turns to helping Christy marry Pegeen in return for favours in the pub.
- She also acts as a role model for the young girls of the play, with her **cunning scheming** and her ability to manipulate Old Mahon, among others.
- She is motivated by **desperation** and the awful prospect of **loneliness**. She will do anything to have a reliable man with her to bring stability and steady income to her household.
- She is still young enough to have numerous children and therefore can be played on stage as a **seductive 'older woman'**, rather than a bitter old widow.
- Nothing works out for her in the end, however. As she leaves the stage in Act 3, she remarks that *'It's in the madhouse they should put him, not the jail,'* as the playboy is led away.

Pegeen Mike – Protagonist 'The Love Interest'	Widow Quin – Antagonist 'The Love Rival'
attractive	scheming
strong-willed	manipulative
quick-thinking	experienced
organised	shrewd
rebellious	realistic
independent	cynical
witty	lonely
outspoken	
disappointed	

Other Characters

The following characters are quite important but are not as complex as the ones above. They are more 'one-dimensional':

- **Old Mahon**
- **Mike Flaherty**
- **Shawn Keogh**

Old Mahon makes a number of appearances and suffers near-death three times in the play.

- **He is the walking embodiment of the lies that Christy tells.** They reconcile just as they are both kicked out of the village.

- However, the play closes with the suggestion that the son has now taken over the dominant position in the family. **Christy calls his father the 'heathen slave'** as they leave.
- The failure of Old Mahon to earn the respect of his son is considered a moral failure on the part of Old Mahon.
- The **violence** that they bring with them is quite real, much less heroic than the tales and legends that they are fond of spreading.

Mike Flaherty is a central character of any rural Irish village, being a publican.

- However, he spends a considerable length of time in the play in various states of drunkenness.
- The drama on his doorstep, and the apparent wildness of his daughter's desires, suggest that he has **lost a grip on authority**. He is not really respected by her.
- In urging Christy and Shawn to literally 'fight for his daughter's hand in marriage,' he demonstrates a level of savagery and brutality that was a source of controversy when the play was first staged.

Shawn Keogh is a **simple, one-dimensional young farmer**, typical of the times.

- He is portrayed in an unflattering light. He is **weak-minded, lacking imagination and terrified of what the priest or bishop might think of him**. He is cowardly, almost to the point of comedy.
- Pegeen boxes his ears at the end, symbolising a lack of connection or attraction between them. It would make their upcoming marriage seem all the more ridiculous.

Themes

1) Family Values

The play asks questions of traditional family values and gender roles at the time.

- All three significant family units suffer from some sort of absence: a) there is no 'Mrs Flaherty' mentioned, so we must assume that Pegeen's mother is dead; b) there is no 'Mrs Mahon' either, for reasons unknown; c) a widow plays a central part in the action.
- When the family unit is damaged or incomplete, it causes difficulty and uncertainty. Rural Irish village life was built upon strong family bonds and values, reinforced by the dominant hand of the Catholic Church. When these things are out of kilter, trouble is bound to happen.
- The Playboy takes advantage of this loose sense of family values. He quickly discovers that a wide range of females – not just Pegeen and the Widow Quin, but also Honor, Sarah, Nelly and Susan – are intrigued by his charms. His interference with the upcoming wedding plans can be seen as partly because the family units

and family values of the village are not upheld strongly enough to put him back in his place.

- The reality for most people in the play is quite simple: life is quite miserable, whereby they are stuck in an environment where one is expected to follow a simple path. Men farm the land, drink and play sports to relax. Women get married at the earliest opportunity and settle into a life of child-rearing and drudgery as 'farmers' wives'. Gossip and illusions of romance fill the women's minds to kill the time. Nothing too exciting happens. The Catholic Church oversees this strict social order, and disobedience – as Shawn tells us regularly – will be punished.

2) Violence and Cruelty

It is remarkable that the village as a whole seems to celebrate the virtue of murdering one's father.

- The playboy 'murderer' is seen as a hero. He is also made a hero at the local sports day. By demonstrating a type of manliness, along with quick wit and poetic charm, the playboy conforms to a basic **stereotype of an ideal boyfriend** and potential husband.
- However, when we see the violence and anger between Christy and Old Mahon 'for real' in Act 3, we get a better reflection of their character. It is no longer a great story but a **bloody and gruesome reality**.
- In order to make life more bearable, the people develop a tremendous sense of imagination and colour in their language and interactions. Many of their observations are **funny but also cruel and sarcastic**. There are countless examples of this in the play and each can be read as an indication of the harshness and cruelty in the minds and hearts of the characters.

Examples

- PEGEEN: *'Marcus Quin, God rest him, got six months for maiming ewes, and he a great warrant to tell stories of Holy Ireland till he'd have the old women shedding down tears about their feet.'* (scolding Shawn for suggesting that there were no 'sinners' in the village)
- SHAWN: *'I'm after feeling a kind of fellow in the furzy ditch, groaning wicked like a maddening dog.'* (upon seeing the playboy on the road earlier)
- MIKE: *'Pegeen, you'll have no call to be spying after if you've a score of young girls weeding in your fields!'* (assuring Pegeen that Shawn is the right man for her)
- CHRISTY: *'I never left my own parish till Tuesday was a week.'* (the playboy's poetic way of saying how long he has been on the run)
- OLD MAHON: *'If he seen a red petticoat coming swinging over the hill, he'd be off to hide in the sticks, and you'd see him shooting out his sheep's eyes between the little twigs and the leaves, and his two ears rising like a hare looking out through a gap. Girls indeed!'* (telling of Christy's true behaviours around young women)

There are many other examples – all of them expressing a great deal of colour and imagination as people try to escape the dull, boring life they actually lead.

exam Q

SAMPLE QUESTION AND ANSWER (10 MARKS/8 MINUTES)

Playboy of the Western World by J. M. Synge (2018)

Question

What does the Widow Quin think of Christy Mahon at the end of the play? Explain briefly and quote from the play.

SAMPLE ANSWER:

When Christie leaves the village at the end of the play, the Widow Quin passes a comment about him and his father, Old Mahon. She says that 'It's in the madhouse they should put him, not the jail.' I think she is actually disappointed by the fact that he didn't fall for her earlier in the play. She tried to seduce him early on and she talked about how good a farmer she was. But Christy didn't really take much interest in her, so by the end of it all she does not care much for him. She is probably a bit jealous too and maybe lonely because she is a widow and for her, a new husband would be very useful for the future.

(125 words)

EXAMINER'S ASSESSMENT

The candidate includes **three possible responses**: disappointed, jealous and lonely. All have some merit but it would be better to **focus more closely** on one or maybe two of these, with supporting reference or quotation. There is sufficient knowledge of the play and the language and mechanics are quite good, so a solid answer, just short of top marks.

MARKS AWARDED

4 + 4 = 8/10 (O2 Grade)

5. *Room* by Emma Donoghue (2019)

Storyline

This novel tells a very dark and disturbing story. It is loosely based on real events, which makes the story even more shocking.

- The narrator of the story is a boy named Jack. It

begins on his fifth birthday. He lives with his mother, who he calls 'Ma', in 'Room', a locked outbuilding containing a small kitchen, a bath and toilet, a wardrobe, a bed, a rug, a TV set and some basic materials. Jack believes that only Room and the things it contains (including himself and Ma) are 'real'. Ma convinces Jack to believe that the rest of the world, or 'Outside', exists only on television. She tries her best to keep Jack healthy and happy and manages a very strict and organised routine for him. She also breastfeeds him regularly.

- 'Old Nick' visits Room at night while Jack sleeps hidden in the wardrobe. Old Nick brings them food and basic things needed to survive. Jack is unaware that Old Nick kidnapped Ma when she was nineteen years old and has kept her locked in Room for the past seven years. Old Nick sexually assaults and rapes Ma regularly. She became pregnant and gave birth to a girl but the baby died while being born. Shortly afterwards, she gave birth to Jack.

- Ma learns that Old Nick has been unemployed for the past six months and is in danger of losing his home. Ma comes up with a plan to get Jack out of Room because she fears that Old Nick might kill them. She pretends that Jack has died and convinces Old Nick to remove him, wrapped in a rug, from Room. Jack then escapes Old Nick and manages to reach a friendly stranger, who contacts the police. He manages to convince the police to find Ma and free her from Room, which they do shortly afterwards.

- Mother and son slowly come to terms with the outside world. It is extremely difficult for both of them to adjust. After a television interview ends badly, Ma suffers a mental breakdown and attempts suicide.

- Jack then goes to live with his grandmother and her new partner for several days. Without the security of his mother, Jack becomes even more confused by his surroundings, including his new extended family. He also becomes more troubled and frightened by his mother's changing personality as she tries to adjust to life. He wants to keep her for himself.

- Finally, Jack cuts his long hair and looks to visit Room once more. He and Ma return to the scene of their captivity, but Jack no longer feels any connection to it. The story ends as he says his goodbyes, touching all of the familiar objects and walls, before he and Ma leave Room together for the final time.

Five Key Words

- **Exposition** – the beginning, introduction, start
- **Complication** – when things go wrong, unwanted changes occur
- **Climax** – the high-point, when tension is at its most heightened
- **Reversal** – when things turn around, a backlash
- **Resolution** – how something ends, resolved, concluded, finished

Some important notes for revising *Room*

- The entire story is told from the **point of view** of a five-year-old. He is the eyes and ears of everything that happens.
- Jack describes things **literally**. (e.g. Jeep; Remote; Meltedy Spoon; Wordy Ball; Skylight; Baby Jesus, etc.) He sees the world as five-year-olds do: in clear, concrete terms, but with a tremendous curiosity.
- This means that many plot details and situations are hinted at and suggested. It **creates a very uncomfortable atmosphere** at times. Perhaps the most disturbing example is how Jack counts the creaks of the bed that are made when Old Nick is assaulting Ma.
- The award-winning film version of the novel is worth watching. But remember that **a film will always be different** to a written text. It tells the story from many angles, unlike the novel.
- It is important to **learn key quotations from the text** and not to rely too heavily on the film.

Five-Part Story

There are five long chapters in the novel. This is similar to a Shakespearean play with five acts:

1) Introduction ('PRESENTS') – we meet Jack, Ma, Old Nick and discover the horror of the situation.
2) Complication ('UNLYING') – Ma is forced to slowly reveal to Jack the truth about 'Outside' and why they are here in Room.
3) Dramatic Climax ('DYING') – Jack escapes from Room by pretending to be dead.
4) Further Complications ('AFTER') – Jack and Ma struggle to adapt and are separated following Ma's attempted suicide.
5) Conclusion ('LIVING') – Jack and Ma are re-united and then visit Room one last time to say goodbye.

A 'Key Moment' in each chapter

1. The first time Jack describes the 'beep-beep' as Old Nick enters Room that night.
2. Jack sees a plane through the skylight and shouts that 'Outside' must be real.
3. Jack escapes in Rug. This episode should be read as one long piece (it is very important).
4. The TV interview – Ma tells their story.
5. Jack cuts his pony-tail and looks forward to meeting Ma again (read from this point to the end).

CHARACTERS

So much of the novel revolves around **Ma** and **Jack**. So in the exam, it is likely that some questions will focus on their relationship and how things change. Here are some broad points about the two of them:

1) Ma

We never get to know her full name but she is portrayed as a truly extraordinary woman.

Ma's Life Story

- She was originally adopted by her parents (Grandma and Grandpa) who are now separated; Grandma's new partner is named Leo.
- She has a brother called Paul, who is married to Deana. They have a child named Bronwyn.
- She describes herself in the interview as 'ordinary' as a child.
- She had an abortion at the age of eighteen.
- She was abducted by Old Nick at nineteen, imprisoned in Room and raped repeatedly.
- She became pregnant with a baby girl who died from suffocation and a lack of proper care during birth.
- The following year, she gave birth to Jack – alone – in Room; the stains from the birth remain on Rug throughout. Jack is attached to the rug and it is an important item for them both.
- She creates the world of 'Room' so that Jack does not have to think about the situation 'Outside'.
- She teaches him everything he needs to know: language, numbers, prayers, hygiene, exercise. She devotes her entire time to keeping him occupied, while trying not to lose her sanity.
- She once tried to kill Old Nick with the lid of the toilet; he broke her wrist in return. She never tried to overpower him after that. She became 'polite'.
- She suffers occasional mental breakdowns and unconsciousness: Jack calls this 'gone'.
- The relationship changes when Jack reaches the age of five. She cannot continue to deny him the truth:
     'What we see on TV is... it's pictures of real things.'
- She makes the decision to fake Jack's death in order to try to escape.
- By doing this she knows that both of their lives are in danger. If it fails, she will likely die an appalling death by starvation.

Ma's Key Moment in the Novel

The TV interview goes very badly. Although she finds it very difficult and has a breakdown, she does tell us many important things:

- Everything she did was for Jack.
- They were never bored together.
- Having a child for herself 'saved' her – she felt that she was 'somebody' and that she was 'alive again'.
- She did everything with Old Nick on 'auto-pilot'.
- Everything was about 'keeping Jack safe'.
- When the world was eleven-foot square, everything was easier to control.
- Doing these things was simply 'being a mother'.
- She insists that they 'escaped' and were not 'rescued'.
- They did it together.

This interview, which appears in the chapter called 'After' is a very important piece of revision. It allows Ma to explain everything from her point of view. This is reported by Jack as narrator – but we get to hear Ma's inner feelings and experiences without Jack interpreting them for us.

- The TV interviewer, and the media in general, want to portray their own version of the story, that somehow Jack and Ma are disturbed and traumatised by being together in this way.
- Ma resists this furiously. It causes her to have a nervous breakdown, meaning Jack must live with his relatives for a time.
- She stops breastfeeding Jack near the end of the novel. This is a major change for Jack but signals the start of a new independent existence, still together, but this time outside of Room.

A True Heroine

The character of Ma is **resilient, creative, patient, caring, understanding, determined, proud** and, in the words of Jack, she has a face that is the *'beautifullest of them all'*. She suffers unspeakable emotional trauma. In spite of this, she is without doubt **a most heroic and admirable young woman, worthy of great praise for what she did.**

2) Jack

The story begins on Jack's fifth birthday.

Jack's Life Story

- Despite what one might expect, he is very similar to most boys of his age:
  — He asks lots of questions.
  — He likes to play games and take exercise.
  — He has a great imagination and likes hearing stories and singing songs.
  — He likes his routine, gets upset if it is disturbed, and is very interested in numbers and counting things properly.

- Naturally, he is incredibly attached to Ma and their separation is very challenging for him.
- He is very thoughtful and kind to his mother, even when she is 'gone' and he is alone and afraid.
- In fact he is quite gifted in a number of ways: his skill with numbers; his memory for poems, stories, songs and prayers; his skills of observation (he notices the mouse and the aeroplane) are excellent.
- Also, he sees the world in concrete terms. He is at an age when that is slowly changing, so trying to understand the adult way of speaking and behaving in 'Outside' is very complicated to him.

Jack's Key Moment in the Novel

- However, his greatest achievement is in managing to escape by playing dead, even to the point of going to the toilet on himself in fear, seriously hurting his knees and getting bitten by a dog, yet not giving away the truth to Old Nick.
- He is just as heroic as Ma; he overcomes the challenge of escaping Old Nick. That is an amazing feat for a five-year-old.
- He overhears something important:

    '...like a newborn in many ways, despite his remarkably accelerated literacy and numeracy.'

    Dr Clay makes this important observation shortly after Jack is admitted for analysis. But because his mother has done an incredible job in raising him, we do not view Jack as being seriously disturbed, wild or 'feral'.

- He has an uneasy relationship with his grandparents, especially Grandpa, who can hardly bear to look at him at first. Grandma does her best but seems to lack empathy and care, despite raising two of her own children.
- He is christened 'Miracle Jack' and 'Bonsai Boy' by the media, a term that Jack thinks is stupid since 'I am not a tree. I am a boy.' Later on, as the doctors refer to five-year-olds as being 'like plastic', he once again needs to point out that 'I am a boy.'
- The fact that he has long hair means that he is mistaken for a girl, another point that annoys him.

Jack's Reaction to 'Outsiders'

- In general, Jack can't really understand the way people in 'Outside' think and speak and he makes one of the funniest and most ironic statements of the whole novel:

    'Outsiders don't understand anything, I wonder do they watch too much television?'

- This suggests that he needs to develop an identity for himself in 'Outside', since other people keep trying to do it for him. The only person who can really help him do this is Ma. Near the end, as he is full of questions, she says to him:
    > *'I will always call you Jack.'*
- When he finally cuts his hair and stops breast feeding, it signals a change in Jack's outlook as he now becomes more comfortable with living in 'Outside'.
- The visit one last time to Room, which now seems so much smaller and uninteresting, signals the real start of his new life together forever with Ma.
- He is just as much the hero of the story as Ma is and is also deserving of great praise.

Other Characters

- **Old Nick** plays his part as the **brutally cruel villain.**
    — We only get some glimpses of him and occasional phrases, recited by Jack as narrator.
    — The 'Room' scenario is enough to convince us that he is a thoroughly awful man, utterly evil in what he is doing.
    — At one stage, he says:
        > *'I figure there must be something wrong... you've never let me get a good look since the day he was born. Poor little freak's got two heads or something.'*
    — He has created a sick, twisted sense of normality and cannot understand why Jack does not accept him.
    — He is caught by the police and we assume he will spend the rest of his life, ironically enough, in a locked cell.
- **Grandma, Steppa, Grandad, Paul** and **Deana** all struggle to relate to Jack as they all enforce their understanding of how things are done in 'Outside'. For example, Jack's trip to the toy store and Grandma's horror at breastfeeding are two good examples of how these adults don't properly understand his needs and end up causing distress for him.
- However, **Officer Oh** (a local policewoman), **Noreen** (an experienced Irish nurse) and **Dr Clay** (the main therapist to Ma) all seem much kinder and understanding towards both Ma and Jack.
- Another neighbour named **Ajeet** is the one who first comes across Jack and he does the correct thing in contacting the police.

Themes

Love

The novel is about the triumph of a mother's love in the face of unspeakable cruelty. It is a story of how love does, after all, conquer evil.

Examples of Love Triumphing

- There is great triumph in the fact that Ma has managed to create a relatively 'normal' life for Jack in Room.
- It is also triumphant that Jack is such a loving, caring and otherwise fairly 'normal' boy, who can also show love back to his mother and, eventually, other people.
- Ma recounts how she gave birth to him alone; she refused to let Old Nick see the birth and managed to keep both herself and her new baby healthy without any post-natal or medical care.
- She is extremely defensive and protective of him in the early stages after release. She tries to assure the doctors that Jack is actually fine: *'He's never been out of my sight and nothing happened to him, nothing like you are insinuating.'*
- Jack is quite healthy, intelligent and enjoys a sound routine. This is entirely down to the tremendous sacrifice and love that Ma afforded to Jack in Room.
- Ma tells her father that Jack *'is the world to me.'* On first seeing Jack, he is lost for words and just utters *'No offence'*, which is probably quite an offensive thing to say in the circumstances.
- The character of Grandpa does not seem the type to respond in the same loving way as Ma does, and blames 'jet lag' for his thinking.
- Ma goes on to explain her love and commitment to Jack in the TV interview. The interviewer asks a question that upsets Ma: she suggests that Ma must *'stand guard between your son and the world.'* Ma responds by saying: *'Yeah, it's called being a mother.'*
- In other words, Ma is saying that any loving mother would do the same. However, very few would be capable of such love and of holding the relationship and their whole world together in the circumstances. Ma does this very successfully for five years.
- **Jack is just as defensive about Ma.** He keeps one of her rotten teeth with him at all times when she is away, even sticking it in his mouth to keep it safe. It is his little way of staying connected to Ma.
- He is also very attached to 'Rug', the way children can be attached to blankets or teddy bears. It is once again his five-year-old way of showing what matters in life.

- What matters most of all is that Ma and himself are together and happy.
- **Steppa** is quite sarcastic at times and suggests to Jack that Ma must know nothing about plumbing. Jack delivers a lovely response, typical of a five-year-old: *'Ma knows about everything.'*
- **The love between Ma and Jack is what lights up the novel.** Any study of this novel cannot miss the theme of love running through it.

The World 'Outside'

A strong theme of the novel is that **the modern world of today can be a scary place.**

- 'Outside' is the world of Old Nick. He lives there comfortably enough and is able to inflict unbelievable cruelty for many years without anybody knowing.
- 'Outside' is also a world where *'people are locked up in all sorts of ways'*, according to Ma. She speaks of babies being tied to cots and prisoners in solitary confinement among other things. She suggests that the world is full of cruelty and suffering and she isn't a 'saint' just because she raised Jack inside Room.
- Their escape also disrupts the routine and 'normality' of Ma and Jack. She has her first proper shower in seven years and tells Jack that *'we don't have to do things as we used to.'*
- But Jack *'likes breakfast before bath'.* She has to stop breastfeeding and Jack must realise that saying and doing certain things and touching people inappropriately, for example, is not acceptable.
- Ma explains the difference between Room and Outside during the interview. She says at one stage that *'when our world was 11-foot square it was easier to control.'* This has a double meaning: Old Nick gets to control their movements but also Ma and Jack get to control how they act together inside there, without any other distractions and influences. Jack also notices the wastefulness of people 'outside' who seem to need enormous amounts of 'stuff' to get through daily life: *'They've got a million of things and different kinds of each thing, like all kinds of chocolate bars and machines and shoes.'* There is an unstated theme here that people can get by together on very little once they learn to value the little that they have.
- Another thing Ma realises on escaping Room is that they are now reluctant 'celebrities'. This is the type of attention neither she nor Jack wants. Her lawyer Morris tries to advise on how best to prepare for the future. He suggests the TV interview and Ma answers: *'You think we should sell ourselves before somebody else does.'*
- Later Jack has to run indoors from the park as a number of paparazzi reporters in helicopters try to get a glimpse of him. His uncle Paul also struggles to disguise Jack's identity when in public, which causes more confusion for Jack.

exam focus

Your notes on characters and themes can help you answer the short 10-mark question on the day. Look at the example on the next page.

- Outside, therefore, is a world where everything is for sale, even the most private intimate details of your most personal intimate relationships.

SAMPLE QUESTION AND ANSWER (10 MARKS/8 MINUTES)

Room by Emma Donoghue (2019)

Question

Explain what happens when Ma and Jack meet Grandpa for the first time. Refer to the text in support of your answer. **(10)**

SAMPLE ANSWER:

The first meeting of the family does not go well. Grandpa has just come off a flight and he says that he has jet-lag. On seeing Jack, he mutters 'no offence'. It is as if he cannot accept what has happened. This is a terrible thing to say in my opinion. Jack as usual does not understand when the adults use words like 'he' and 'me' so he gets confused at this time. Ma on the other hand explodes with anger and reminds her father that Jack 'is the world to me'. It is a sad moment for Ma once again because it shows us that people in 'outside' find it really difficult to adapt to the needs of Ma and her son Jack. Her father can't even say he is glad to see her in this moment.

(138 words)

EXAMINER'S ASSESSMENT

This is a concise and detailed answer that addresses the question and demonstrates good knowledge of the moment in question. Two accurate quotations with following explanation, well-phrased with good vocabulary, mean that this will score highly in the exam.

MARKS AWARDED

6 + 4 = 10/10 (O1 Grade)

6. *Circle of Friends* by Maeve Binchy (2019)

Storyline

Circle of Friends focuses on **Benny Hogan** and **Eve Malone**, two close friends who live in a small Irish village called **Knockglen**.

Early Days

- Although they have grown up together, their circumstances are quite different. Benny is the only child of over-protective parents, while Eve's parents died when she was an infant. She has been raised by the loving nuns in the local Catholic convent.

- Both retain some **resentment*** – Benny toward her parents' excessive control, and Eve toward the Westwards, the influential family who disowned her mother. They believe that she married badly and below her **status*** and then had to abandon Eve when she was orphaned.

- Chapter 1 is set in 1949 when Benny is ten; the rest of the novel is set eight years later when she goes to college in Dublin.

The Move to Dublin

- Benny's parents have saved enough money to send her to University College Dublin, but they demand that she return home to Knockglen each night. There is not enough money to send Eve to college so it has been arranged for her to live at a Dublin convent while doing a secretarial course.

- Eve longs for a college education and the university experience, so she eventually swallows her pride and asks her cousin, Simon Westward, to pay for it, and to her surprise he agrees.

A Dramatic Beginning

- A freak car accident on the first day of college takes the life of student Frank Hegarty and injures Eve, but it also brings the girls together with fellow students Nan Mahon and Jack Foley, who are also connected to the incident.

- Nan is stunningly beautiful and, encouraged by her mother, plans to escape her modest home and alcoholic father by marrying well. Jack is the charming, handsome son of a local doctor. Together they form a close circle that includes several other students.

Benny's First Love?

- Soon Benny attracts the attention of the sought-after Jack and begins a relationship with him. This development also surprises Sean Walsh, a young man who works in Benny's father's menswear shop and plans to **inherit*** the business by marrying Benny. This idea pleases her parents, who cannot see any different future for Benny, but she is not so sure.

- As the university life in Dublin blends with life in Knockglen, Nan meets Simon Westward, Eve's cousin, and begins planning a future with him. What Nan does not realise is that the Westwards are no longer wealthy and while Simon is **infatuated*** by her beauty, he is also shopping around for a wife who can bring a significant amount of money into the marriage.

Things Get Complicated

- Nan becomes pregnant, and is shocked when Simon ends the relationship by giving her money for an abortion.
- In the meantime, Benny's father dies suddenly, and she feels the need to spend more time in Knockglen, which frustrates Jack.
- Nan takes advantage of the situation and begins secretly seeing Jack, eventually telling him she is pregnant and implying she was a virgin when they began sleeping together. He feels **obligated*** to marry her, and they get engaged, breaking Benny's heart and shocking all of their friends.

Things Fall Apart

- At a party, Eve realises what has happened and confronts Nan, who falls into a glass door and is seriously injured. She recovers but miscarries. She and Jack end their relationship.
- Sean marries Mrs Healy back in Knockglen and they work together in the local hotel.
- Simon Westward plans a marriage to a wealthy English woman.

Friends to the End

- Jack tries to reconcile with Benny, but she has now moved beyond her attraction to him and is able to see him simply as a member of their circle of friends.
- The two closest friends, Benny and Eve, decide to 'share a flat next year' in Dublin as their friendship endures the challenges they both have faced in their lives so far, especially during the course of the previous year.

Five Key Words

- **Resentent** – a strong dislike, rejection, distaste
- **Status** – position in society, standing, reputation
- **Inheritance** – received from ancestors, valuables passed on
- **Infatuated** – obsessed, an unhealthy level of attraction
- **Obligated** – obliged, necessitated, what 'must be done'

Some important notes on revising *Circle of Friends*

- This is a long novel – but it is mostly a story of **friendship, love and the search for happiness**, especially in the journeys of Benny and Eve.
- Money, or **'financial security'**, is also an important issue for many of the characters.
- It is best to focus on a **selection of key moments** in the novel as these will likely form the exam questions on the day:
  — **the car crash;**
  — **Benny and Jack walking together;**

— the party night in Chapter 10;
— Eve's party in her cottage during Christmas;
— Benny's father's death;
— Nan's break-up with Simon;
— the row between Nan and Eve in Chapter 19;
— the conclusion.

Written text v film version: WARNING!

The film version made in 1995 is worth watching. However, there are some significant **DIFFERENCES** to the text:

- Mother Francis and Kit Hegarty are not included in the film.
- Nan is not a childhood friend of Benny; they meet in UCD in the novel.
- Sean stays in Knockglen in the novel – he marries Mrs Healy eventually and they run the local hotel.
- There is no physical confrontation between Sean and Benny and he does not attempt to sexually assault her. This is a key moment in the film but is NOT in the novel.

key point

Do not depend entirely upon a film version in order to prepare for an exam on a written text.

CHARACTERS

The six characters that form the basis of most revision are:

- Benny
- Eve
- Nan
- Jack
- Simon
- Sean

Exam questions are likely to be based upon these characters.

1) Benny Hogan – likeable, awkward, genuine

Bernadette or 'Benny' is the **likeable** girl who is the central character in the novel. She is depicted as *'large and square'* in her youth, which makes her **self-conscious** as she matures. She considers herself 'so big and drab looking', as she heads to college aged eighteen. She is also **affectionate, warm-hearted and generous,** mostly as a result of her upbringing in Knockglen, where she is taught to see the good in people. Her parents are conservative and over-protective, but are **essentially good people** who manage a successful village clothing store. Throughout the various key moments, Benny seeks to act justly and to **do the right thing**, while trying to look after her own interests. Sometimes this works against her. Some examples:

- Her biggest mistake is in thinking there is 'nothing to worry about', while her two friends Nan and Jack carry on an affair behind her back. This is the most important lesson she learns in the novel – that **people can be cruel, jealous and devious**, even those close to you.
- Sean dismisses her love for Jack as 'infatuation'. She makes the mistake of confiding in him in the first place. (ch. 13)
- After the car accident she is more worried about Eve and the other injured than herself. (ch. 4)
- When her father dies suddenly in the middle of the novel, she feels that she must take responsibility for the family business, even if this means losing out on a life in Dublin. (ch. 14)

But Benny shows a **determination** and a **strong sense of character** throughout the novel:

- She is suspicious of Nan and does not want to allow her to see Eve in the hospital so as to protect Eve's privacy. (ch. 5)
- She manages to expose Sean for the greedy fraudster that he is by confronting him directly. (ch. 16)
- She is careful not to fall completely for Jack at first; she is aware of her feelings for him, however.
- Kissing him for the first time is like *'the most natural thing in the world.'* However, she is more of a 'companion' to him than a true lover. (ch. 12)
- She shows that she is more assertive and confident at the end by refusing to take Jack back; while she is somewhat sad, she knows it is right as he is unreliable and likely to be unfaithful. She feels now that his presence is *'not taking over the whole night sky.'*

2) Eve Malone – loyal, faithful, strong-willed

Eve plays the part of the best friend. She has had an unusual upbringing, being orphaned and then reared in a convent by nuns, watched over by the caring and good-natured Mother Francis. By the end of the story, **she is the person who is closest to Benny**, even more so than before. They are *'staying some nights in Dun Laoghaire together and other nights both went home.'*

- She is quite pretty – Aidan Lynch takes a shine to her – but she is not ready for a relationship.
- She shows good judgement – not just regarding Nan but also in controlling her own life as she matures.
- She forces Simon Westward into paying for her education.

- She refuses to stay in the Dublin convent as she is not treated properly.
- She befriends both Kit Hegarty and her cousin Heather Westward and is generally a positive influence on other people's lives.
- Eve flies to Benny's defence, attacking Nan and injuring her during the party scene – this is in tribute to Benny who always defended her in school.
- She moves into the 'small cottage' once owned by her mother. The fact that she ends up there is very satisfying for her as the supposedly wealthy Westwards sit in a pool of debt abroad in the big house. (*'Westward owed Shea's since last Christmas for the drink he had bought'*)

Eve is an independent, strong-willed and admirable character, the type of best friend we would all benefit from.

3) Nan Mahon – attractive, selfish, troubled

Unfortunately for Nan, she is a **villain,** mostly because she is motivated almost entirely by self-interest.

- All through the novel, Nan is described as being very attractive with words like '**stunning**' and '**dazzling**' used repeatedly. Her beauty was not just the opinion of her own mother but *'this was the opinion of everyone.'*
- She feels that she should get ahead in life by any means possible, which involves lying to everybody else in the novel and using other people, most especially Eve and her cottage, to get what she wants.
- She is a **troubled** person. She has many issues in her life which are covered up by her outward beauty and her apparent happiness.
- She has an alcoholic father and an unhappy home life.
- She thinks that marrying a Westward will improve her status in society, despite Simon Westward being almost penniless.
- She fakes most of her friendship with Eve; it is purely because of the family connection that she is interested.
- When it turns out that Simon will not continue their relationship, she manipulates Jack, even to the point of telling him he is the father of her unborn child.
- She cares little for the feelings of the other characters – she even ends up engaged to a man for whom she has no genuine love.
- She disappears at the end of the novel to an uncertain future.

Ultimately, **Nan is a very flawed character** for whom we may have some sympathy. She has come from a difficult home environment and has grown up with young men constantly admiring her and telling her she is beautiful. But her flaw is that she continually thinks she is better than everybody around her.

4) Jack Foley – handsome, foolish, weak

Jack comes from a life of privilege as the son of a doctor. It helps that he is also very handsome and has very fine social skills. But Jack is **far from a hero**. In fact, he is **quite a fool**.

- Early on, Nan remarks that *'he's the college hero even before he gets there'*, seeing that he has already played schools rugby and was 'very good'.
- However, he is used to things being 'easy' in life and is **unused to hardship**, hard decisions or dealing with challenging people.
- He is **weak-willed and shallow**. This is best seen in the way he is easily manipulated by Nan, almost to the point of marrying her.
- He treats Benny poorly in the story. He **'walks companionably'** with her, knowing she has affection for him. But he shows more interest in Rosemary Ryan.
- He then starts to spend more time with Benny, kissing her *'as if it was the most natural thing in the world'*. But he also has an affair with a 'brainless blonde' before being easily charmed by Nan on the rebound from Simon.
- He even goes back to Benny at the end, but she at least has the resolve to reject his advances.

Jack is the sort of privileged young male who may appear charming and admirable on the outside, but is in fact a shallow and two-faced individual at heart.

5) Simon Westward – shallow, selfish, blunt

Simon is portrayed negatively in the novel as a member of a particular social class. He is a 'leftover' of the old wealthy Protestant community in Ireland, a family associated with the 'big house' of rural areas.

- He seems almost **entirely concerned with wealth**, status and retaining a sense of superiority over others.
- When Nan asks Simon if he is a fortune-hunter, he says *'Of course I am.'* There is a degree of **honesty** in Simon. It is easy to understand his motives, even if they are narrow and ruthless. He seems to **lack care or empathy** for others.

Simon's Money

- Money is the solution for all of his issues:
  - He sends Heather to boarding school, thus preventing her from having any influence.
  - He sends Nan 'away' with a cheque for an abortion.
  - He pays for Eve's education, ensuring that she goes 'away' and does not come looking for any inheritance.

— He continually fails to pay for the drinks in the village pub. This does not concern him: such people as the publicans would be considered beneath him in importance.

— He ends up marrying a rich English woman so as to save the family estate. This was always his intention, regardless of his affairs with others in the novel.

In conclusion, Simon Westward is a straightforward, uncomplicated and quite unlikeable character in the novel.

6) Sean Walsh – scheming, deceitful, desperate

Sean Walsh is the one who has **no redeeming feature or admirable trait** at all. There is nothing to make him appealing whatsoever.

- He is regularly described in unpleasant terms, such as **'thin', 'pale' 'calculating'** and his motivations are always questionable.
- He has ambition to succeed in business, but he does so by scheming and stealing from the Hogan's business for years.
- His interest in Benny is purely so as to take over the family business in time.
- He spreads gossip and rumour – he puts fear in Benny's mother's head after the crash, for example.
- He dismisses the genuine thoughts of Benny and her love for Jack as 'infatuation' when he would be better off saying nothing.
- He returns to Knockglen after being exposed for the financial fraud that he is and proposes marriage to Mrs Healy of the local hotel. They marry in Rome, away from the support of the local community.

There is nothing to make Sean Walsh appealing as a character. But he has an important role in the novel as a character who is **ruthless and selfish in seeking what he wants**, while pretending to be 'friendly' and polite on the surface. Unfortunately for Sean, nobody really buys this in the end, except Mrs Healy.

Themes

Love

The novel deals with various types of love and how characters react to the various experiences of love that they have.

Parental Love

- Eddie and Annabel Hogan certainly do love their daughter dearly. However, they struggle with the idea of letting her go to college and leave home for the first time. Benny remarks that *'they had behaved as if she were a toddler going to a first party.'* It proves that they care deeply for her, even if it seems a bit over-protective.

- Benny's return to the family home on her father's death is partly out of love and devotion to her father, who reared her so well in the first place, and partly out of the need to be there for her mother at that time.
- Eve's father, we are told, had worked many years for the convent before he died. In part payment for his duty, Mother Francis had reared the orphaned Eve much like her own child. Also, there had *'never been any pressure on Eve to join the order'*. This resulted in Eve growing up to be the young woman that she appears to be in the novel, loyal and devoted like her father.
- Nan has never properly experienced love from her abusive father; it explains to a degree why she seems quite desperate in the novel to rise above others and be seen with 'better people'. She confuses love, friendship and loyalty with beauty, image and outward appearances.

Romantic Love

- Romantic love, particularly between Benny and Jack, holds much of the story together. Jack's failure to remain faithful to Benny shows how this **romantic love can very easily go wrong**. He betrays her a number of times, most especially with Nan.
- Sean Walsh has a particular understanding of love: he sees **love and romance in business terms**, closely linked to the contract of marriage. In fact, his real love is for material things, such as the money and power a marriage might bring. His supposed interest in Benny is so that he can take over the family business. He ends up married to Mrs Healy and a partner in the hotel business.

Money

It is noticeable that many of the characters in the novel have issues around money, one way or another.

- The Westwards, especially Simon, are not nearly as rich as they seem; they also disowned Eve's mother based upon her choice of husband.
- The Mahon family are troubled by alcoholism: 'it was easier to run a hotel shop than to run a family' remarks Nan's mother Emily.
- Sean Walsh is desperate to make his fortune; he has also been stealing from the Hogans for years.
- The convent puts money together for Eve to go to Dublin as she has no source of income.
- Eve then needs money from Simon to attend college.
- Nan is given money to have an abortion: for Simon, money will solve all problems.
- Jack and Benny's relationship fails, partly because they come from very different social classes; his family is quite wealthy while Benny's are small country business people. He does not seem to truly respect this part of Benny's world.

Financial Security Rather than just 'Money'

- A better way to put this is to consider the word **'security'**, which means having enough money to keep you happy and safe at any given time.

- Some characters – the Westwards, the Foleys, Sean Walsh, Nan – see money as defining 'who you are'. They are insecure if there isn't money to keep and maintain their lifestyle. They put selfish interests ahead of other people.

- On the other hand, things like friendship and loyalty are more important than money in the eyes of some characters – Benny, Eve and Heather Westwood for example. **Their happiness and security is not defined by how much money they have.**

exam focus

Your notes on characters and themes can help you answer the short 10-mark question on the day. Look at the example below.

---

exam Q

SAMPLE QUESTION AND ANSWER (10 MARKS/8 MINUTES)

Circle of Friends **by Maeve Binchy**

What sort of character is Sean Walsh in *Circle of Friends*? Explain and refer to the text in your answer. **(10)**

SAMPLE ANSWER:

> Sean Walsh is not a likeable character in the novel. He is described as being pale, thin and calculating which makes him look like an unpleasant ugly man. He treats everybody very badly most especially the Hogan family who have employed him for years. After Benny's father dies, he continues to interfere in the business and each week he has been taking money from them. Benny stands up to him, along with her mother, in chapter 16. He cannot accept that he has been caught but eventually he has to leave and go work with Mrs Healy in the local hotel. He is greedy and selfish and even manages to be cruel to Benny along the way, laughing at her infatuation over Jack. Sean Walsh is a villain in this novel.
>
> (132 words)

EXAMINER'S ASSESSMENT

There are a number of points made here, all relevant. However, the answer would benefit from the placing of key adjectives – greedy, selfish, cruel – at the start and the use of quotation thereafter. Vocabulary and expression are adequate and basic. Otherwise, it is a solid answer for 10 marks.

MARKS AWARDED

4 + 3 = 7/10 (O3 Grade)

7 The Comparative Study

aims
- To understand the **modes of comparison**.
- To learn a **method of revision** for this section, understanding the **importance of comparisons as well as contrasts**.

- The Comparative Study is worth **70 marks** – this equals 17.5% of the entire exam.
- You should spend about **60–65 minutes** on this section in total.
- Your class will have covered **at least two and maybe even three texts** for this part of the course.
- Every school is different so be **absolutely clear** on **which texts** you have studied.
- You **CANNOT use the 'Single Text'** again in this section.
- These texts can be a **combination** of novels, plays, autobiographies, a film or some other form of text.
- You do **NOT** have to have covered a text by **SHAKESPEARE** – this is compulsory for Higher Level but is **optional for you at Ordinary Level**.
- However, it is very likely that you will have studied a **FILM** – so that becomes an **important part of this section**.

17.5%

What Must I Do in the Exam?

In simple terms, you must answer a series of questions based upon your texts, under certain headings or 'Modes of Comparison'. They are outlined here:

2018 EXAM	–	Social Setting
		Relationships
		Hero, Heroine, Villain
2019 Exam	–	Theme
		Relationships
		Hero, Heroine Villain

Structure of the comparative study section

Use the **3–2–1 formula** for remembering how the Comparative Study section is structured on your exam paper.

- **Three** modes of comparison are prescribed for each year.
- **Two** will appear on the exam paper.
- **One** question – **parts (a) and (b)** – is all that you must do.

Identify which modes are relevant for your year of examination and **thoroughly revise two modes.** This is sufficient to have you prepared for the exam.

Some other points to remember when preparing for this section of the exam:

- You cannot just tell the story of your chosen texts. The purpose of this section is to **test your skills of comparison.**
- This means being able to spot aspects of the texts that are similar. It also involves highlighting differences. You are asked to **compare and contrast** and that is what you are marked on.
- The best approach is not to revise all of the material in each text. Instead, focus on a number of **key moments** in each text, which will provide you with the material for exam answers.
- Key moments are often moments of revelation, discovery, choice, tension or climax. Key moments often bring about some kind of change.
- Experience shows that **the same key moments in a text often work with any of the modes.** Be careful in choosing moments or scenes; ensure that they have a major bearing on the story.
- **Be very careful not to confuse the Single Text with the Comparative Texts.** This will lead to automatic disqualification of marks by the examiner.
- At Ordinary Level, you **do not have to study Shakespeare** for the Comparative Study section.

Film

The inclusion of film on the Comparative Study section has proven to be very popular. Films can be studied just like any other text, but it is worth noting these points:

- Films **show** you a story; they don't just tell you something. The **theme** of a film is contained in what you see and hear.
- Look carefully at how **colour** is used for effect.
- Be aware of how **sound** and **music** influence your reaction to the story and characters. This includes the soundtrack and the musical score (background or incidental music).
- Films are always located in a certain place and time, a **social setting** with a particular atmosphere.

- Look at how **actors** behave at key moments. How are relationships shaped and developed?
- Films contain great moments of **tension** and **climax**. Know when these occur and remember the resolution (how it all ends).
- Consider from whose **point of view** we see the action unfold. What are we being shown? What or who can we not see?
- What is the main **theme** of the film? All film-makers have something to tell us, which is shown in the work they create. Know exactly what that point is before continuing to revise for your exam. Start by jotting down the main themes of your studied film.

Questions asked

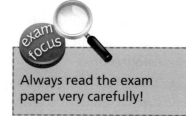

Two **modes** will appear on your exam paper. It is likely that you will also have a **choice within the mode**: an A or B option. For example, if you choose to do the **Theme** mode, you will have **two sets of questions** and **you must do one.**

Always read the exam paper very carefully!

The exam questions are usually split into **two parts**, with the marks divided 30/40:

- The **30-mark question** usually asks about a **mode** of comparison in **one** text.
- The **40-mark question** will require a longer answer. This is where the real business of **comparison with another text (or texts)** takes place.

30-mark questions

The 30-mark questions usually appear as part (a) of a two-part question. You will most likely be asked to write about one text. **You should practise doing short essays (200–300 words) on different modes appearing in one text.**

Recent 30-mark exam questions include the following:

- Name a **theme** from one of your comparative texts. Show how this theme plays an important part in the story.
- Describe **one significant relationship** in one of your chosen texts.
- Choose one of your comparative texts and **outline a relationship that had a strong impact** on you.
- Describe the **social setting** of one of your comparative texts and say whether or not it appealed to you.
- Choose a **person** from one of your texts in your comparative course whose **behaviour you admired or did not admire** and write a short account of him or her.

40-mark questions

The 40-mark questions usually appear as part (b) of a two-part question. **They require you to compare what you have written in (a) to another text you have studied.** You must stick to the question asked and remember your key moments.

Recent 40-mark exam questions include the following:

- Show how the **same theme** was **portrayed differently** in another text from your course.
- Choose a **relationship from another text which was different to the one outlined in (a)**. Say what made this relationship different.
- Choose a **relationship from another text** from your course. Explain **what was different about the impact** this had on you.
- Describe **the social setting of another text** from your comparative studies and show the **similarities and/or differences** that you found when compared to the text in (a). Refer to each text in making your points.
- Choose a **character from another text** from your comparative course. **Compare him or her with the person you have chosen in (a) and say which of the two you preferred.**

POINTS TO NOTE:

One of the things that is very important at this stage of the exam is to READ the paper as carefully as possible. It is time well spent so as to make a good choice. This question carries the most marks in Paper 2, so be careful in making your decision.

- **KNOW** the name of your texts and the author/director, etc.
- **READ** the questions very carefully.
- **IDENTIFY** the task in each one.
- **UNDERLINE** the keywords in each one.
- **DECIDE** which mode you will answer on (we will choose **'relationships'** in the example below).
- **CHOOSE** either number 1 or number 2. Cross out all other questions just to be sure.
- **PLAN** your response:
  — 5 minutes rough work;
  — 12 minutes × 2 for the 15-mark questions;
  — 30 minutes on the 40-mark question;
  — 5 minutes re-reading and correcting at the end.
- **TOTAL TIME = 65 minutes maximum!**

Preparing for the exam

The first thing a student must do to revise the Comparative Study is to ask: **which is my favourite text?** Consider the two or three Comparative Texts you have studied (do not include your Single Text)

Of all the sections in Paper 2, the Comparative Study section requires the most careful reading of the questions.

and choose one to use as a base or anchor for your answers. Once you have examined an anchor text and a second text in this way, you have the **raw material for any question** that can appear on your exam paper.

Be sure to **include the names** of your **chosen texts and their authors/directors every time** you answer an exam question.

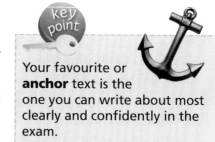

Your favourite or **anchor** text is the one you can write about most clearly and confidently in the exam.

REVISION – all about the 'KEY MOMENTS'

Good exam revision is based around a selection of **key moments** in your text.

- They are typically found at the **start** and the **end** of the text, as well as **turning points, moments of tension** or a '**climax**' of some sort.
- Make a list of these for each of your chosen texts. It is likely that **these moments will be central** to any of the questions asked on the paper.
- **Seven or eight moments** is usually enough for revision purposes.
- These moments – with **quotations** – are what you need to revise.

Revise thoroughly **two** of the modes prescribed for the year of your exam.

EXAMPLE – how to structure your revision for Comparative Studies Questions

1) FIRST TEXT = *Children of Men* (dir. Alfonso Cuarón)

Key Moment/Scene	Important Quotations
Opening sequence up to the bombing of the coffee shop	• 'Day 1000 in the siege of Seattle' (voiceover) • 'Deportation of illegal immigrants will continue' • 'Diego Ricardo was 18 years, 4 months, 30 days, 16 hours and 8 minutes old'
Theo is abducted by the Fishes and meets Julian	• 'The Fishes are at war with the British Government until they recognise equal rights for every immigrant in Britain' (Theo, interrogated) • 'What exactly do you guys do anyway' (Theo) • 'We need transit papers' (Julian to Theo – outlining the quest that Theo must eventually undertake)

Key Moment/Scene	Important Quotations
The 'Ark of the Arts' scene with cousin Nigel	• 'In His anger, He has taken away from us, His most precious gift!' (Preacher, explaining human infertility) • 'The thing is, I met this girl' (Theo, lying about why he is there) • 'Transit papers? That's quite a favour' (Nigel, in reply) • 'I just don't think about it' (Nigel explains how he deals with the upcoming end of humanity)
Theo and Kee meet – their car is then attacked	• 'This is obviously the elite unit' (Theo, sarcastically) • 'You told me he was suave. The wanker's a drunk' (Kee's impression of Theo) • 'I'm not gonna make it!' (Luke, while the car is attacked)
Discovering that Kee is pregnant and escaping that night	• 'I'm scared' and 'Please help me' (Kee, revealing that she is pregnant) • 'Jesus Christ!' (Theo, in response) • 'This baby is the flag that can unite us all' (one of The Fishes' demands that Kee stay with them) • 'Make it public!' (Theo's preference for Kee) • 'We will find a way to get you to the Human Project, I promise you' (Luke, pleading with Kee) • 'They want your baby', 'We have to leave' and 'Trust me, we have to go' (Theo realises the danger)

Key Moment/Scene	Important Quotations
Meeting with Syd	• 'As the sound of the playgrounds faded, the despair set in' (Miriam, remembering when the crisis began) • 'She's not gonna puke is she? Puking's bad. Very bad. (Syd) • 'Syd doesn't want to know. Syd doesn't care' (Syd's attitude to everybody in general)
Theo, Kee and the baby walk through the war zone	• 'Look at that, Theo. They love my baby!' (proud new mother Kee) • 'Human Project – real?' (Theo is asked if it is true) • 'Allahu Akbar!' or 'God is Great' in Arabic (the marching, protesting crowd) • 'Kee. Thank God. You will be safe now.' (Luke, pretending to support Kee) • 'Look around you. It's the uprising!' (Luke to Theo) • 'I'd forgotten what they looked like; they are so beautiful.' (Luke, about to die, having tried to take the baby)
They escape on a small boat	• 'What a day!' (Theo) • 'Trust me. They will come back' (Theo) • 'Just tap her back. Gently' (Theo, showing Kee how to care for the crying baby) • 'Dylan. I will call my baby Dylan. It's a girl's name too' (Kee, in tribute to Theo)

2) SECOND TEXT = *Big Maggie* John B. Keane

Key Moment/Scene	Important Quotations
The opening: Maggie and Byrne discuss the funeral	• 'The day you wrong me Byrne is the day you get me pregnant' (Maggie) • 'There's enough lies written on the headstones of Ireland without me adding to them' (Maggie) • 'You'll turn out like your father if you aren't careful' (Maggie, to Gert)

Key Moment/Scene	Important Quotations
Katie enters; Maggie is not very sympathetic (Act 1, scene 1)	• 'Anyone that abused you ended up second in the long run' (Mick, to Maggie) • 'There's a time coming when you won't have much to say for yourself' (Maggie to Katie) • 'I'd say she won't think of the next world till the day she enters it' (Byrne, reflecting on Maggie)
Mick exits and vows not to return (Act 1, scene 2)	• 'You're mad if you think I'm going to stay here for pocket money' (Mick, to Maggie) • 'I'm in no position to guarantee anything to anybody' (Maggie, to her children) • 'My father is a lucky man to be free of you' (Mick, to Maggie as he leaves)
Maggie violently confronts Katie and forces her to marry (Act 1, scene 2)	• 'Have I raised a whore!' (Maggie, to Katie) • 'I'll beat you so that your own sister won't know you' (Maggie, again) • 'I was committing a sin with him.' and 'I couldn't help myself' (Katie, to Maggie) • 'I thought you were more brazen, more of a woman. You're still a child' (Maggie, in reply)
Gert sees Maggie and Teddy kissing (Act 2, scene 1)	• 'I thought about you all day' (Teddy, to Maggie) • 'You're so uncomplicated' (Maggie, to Teddy) • 'She'll get over it and won't travel the same road I did' (Maggie, regarding Gert) • 'If a man or woman hasn't self-respect, they have nothing' (Maggie, to Teddy)

Key Moment/Scene	Important Quotations
Maurice confronts Maggie demanding to marry Mary Madden (Act 2, scene 2)	• 'The day she lobs £1500 on the counter I'll be the first one to dance at her wedding' (Maggie, concerning Mary Madden) • 'You have no training for anything but the pick and shovel' (Maggie, to Maurice) • 'And will you be in love with her when she's trying to rear three or four children in a poke of a flat' (Maggie, again) • 'I've given my whole life to that farm and this is what I get in the end' (Maurice, in reply)
Maggie and Mrs Madden argue (Act 2, scene 3)	• 'Come down off your high horse missus or you'll be a sorry woman' (Mrs. Madden, to Maggie) • 'The cheek of you to come barging into my house like a circus elephant!' (Maggie, in reply)
Maggie's final speech, alone on stage (Conclusion)	• 'I'm alone now and I'm free and not too many women can say that'

Putting Answers Together

By re-reading these parts (suggested by the texts above) and memorising the quotations, it then becomes possible to answer questions on one or other of the MODES on the day. Break your own texts down in this fashion. The same approach is useful, no matter what text you have studied.

Third Text?

If your teacher has studied a **third text** during fifth or sixth year, then once again fill out the key moments in your own words. Use the box below as a guide.

Text = ...

Key Moments	Quotations

IMPORTANT!

Exam answers sometimes ask that you refer to 'at least two texts.' This means that **TWO IS ENOUGH**.

Choose the **two that you enjoyed the most** and answer the questions based upon them.

Choosing Questions on the Day

Read the following questions on 'Relationships' taken from the 2016 examination.

This mode will be examined in 2018 and in 2019.

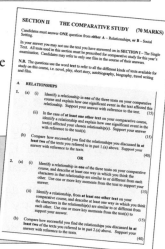

If you look at the exam paper, you might notice that there is a huge volume of information to be read in this section.

So READ THESE QUESTIONS CAREFULLY. This is very important at this stage of the exam when you are likely to be tired.

SECTION II THE COMPARATIVE STUDY (70 MARKS) 2016 Exam

Candidates must answer ONE question from either (a) – Relationships, or (b) – Social Setting. In your answer you may not use the text you have answered on in SECTION I – The Single Text. All texts used in this section must be prescribed for comparative study for this year's examination. Candidates may refer to only one film in the course of their answers. N.B. The questions use the word text to refer to all the different kinds of texts available for study on this course, i.e. novel, play, short story, autobiography, biography, travel writing and film.

A – 'RELATIONSHIPS'

1. (a) (i)   Identify a relationship in one of the three texts on your comparative course and explain how one significant event in the text affected this relationship. Support your answer with reference to the text. **(15)**

    (ii) In the case of at least one other text on your comparative course, identify a relationship and explain how one significant event in the text(s) affected your chosen relationship(s). Support your answer with reference to the text(s). **(15)**

    (b) Compare how successful you find the relationships you discussed in at least two of the texts you referred to in part (a) above. Support your answer with reference to the texts. **(40)**

    OR

2. (a) (i)   Identify a relationship in one of the three texts on your comparative course, and describe at least one way in which you think the characters in

that relationship are similar to or different from each other. Use one or more key moments from the text to support your answer. **(15)**

(ii) Identify a relationship, from at least one other text on your comparative course, and describe at least one way in which you think the characters in the relationship(s) are similar to or different from each other. Use one or more key moments from the text(s) to support your answer. **(15)**

(b) Compare how successful you find the relationships you discussed in at least two of the texts you referred to in part (a) above. Support your answer with reference to the texts. **(40)**

Answering the Comparative Study Question

- We will answer Question 1 above and will do so by examining closely a SIGNIFICANT EVENT ('Key moment') from each and then comparing how successful each relationship was.
- Note closely how just **ONE** key moment from **ONE** relationship is needed; revising these **KEY MOMENTS** and remembering quotations is the way to revise, whatever your chosen text is.
- Examiners are looking for '**comparative vocabulary**', which is language that clearly compares one text with another. **See the list of useful phrases at the end of this chapter.**

SAMPLE ANSWER:

1. (a) (i)   I have studied the film *Children of Men*, directed by Alfonso Cuarón and *Big Maggie* by John B. Keane. In the film, the relationship between Theo and Kee is very important because they are the protagonists and they have the future of the human race in their hands.
The scene where they first meet is a significant moment. Julian has persuaded Theo to take on the dangerous task of helping Kee escape from England to the Human Project. They jump into a car along with Miriam and Luke and are told that once they get to the first checkpoint they are '**on their own.**'

Theo is very unimpressed. He is sarcastic and dismissive. He calls the group in the car '**obviously the elite unit**'. Kee looks at him and snaps '**the fuck you starin**' at?' It is a very tense and unhappy moment for them both. Kee is very unimpressed with Theo as she expected him to be '**suave**'. They don't really want to be there and neither of them is looking forward to the future.

It is a little later when we discover why they are together as Kee is pregnant and needs to be saved from danger. When their car is attacked, Julian is shot and dies. This changes everything as now Theo and Kee are on the run from the police and army. Whether they like each other or not, it now means that they must work together to keep the human race alive.

It is a really significant moment. The relationship started very badly but now they rely on each other for survival.

(268 words)

EXAMINER'S ASSESSMENT

This is an excellent answer. The candidate provided important plot details and then explains clearly why it is a significant moment, along with supporting quotation. The language and mechanics are of a very high standard.

MARKS AWARDED

9 + 6 = 15/15 (O1 Grade)

(ii)   In *Big Maggie* the scene where Maggie confronts Kate about her affair with Toss Melch is very significant. Maggie argues with Kate, telling her that **'you haven't a penny to your name without my say so'**. Maggie knows that Kate had done something upstairs in a hotel room with Toss Melch. He is a married man so in effect Maggie accuses Kate of a sexual sin. She threatens to **'break this brush across your back'** if she doesn't tell the truth. Maggie goes on to say **'have I raised a whore?'** after which she slaps her face and pulls her by the hair. Kate eventually breaks down in tears and cries out that **'I couldn't help myself'**. Maggie tells her to **'Get up and act like a woman'**.

This is a significant moment that affected their relationship because now Maggie has broken the spirit of Kate and she will have to obey her. Kate was very fond of her father so this sometimes put her in opposition to her mother. Maggie forces Kate to marry Johnny Conlan so this makes an 'honest woman' of her 'whore' of a daughter. This changes everything for Kate and Maggie. From this moment on, Maggie controls how Kate will act, which prevents her from challenging Maggie's position as head of the family.

(225 words)

EXAMINER'S ASSESSMENT

This candidate shows an **excellent knowledge** of the scene with the use of numerous quotations. The **question is addressed** perfectly and the language of the question – 'significant moment', 'affect the relationship' – is used when answering. Language and mechanics are of a very good standard.

MARKS AWARDED

9 + 6 = 15/15 (O1 Grade)

(b) (i) (NOTE: key comparative language is highlighted)

I think that **both relationships** were successful but the one between Theo and Kee was the **more successful of the two**. *Children of Men* involves a journey to freedom for Theo and Kee. Along the way, a baby is born. **Similarly**, Big Maggie shows a family on a journey to the future after the death of their father. A baby is **also** born to Kate during this time. Yet **the big difference** is that Theo and Kee are much closer as a result of their journey together, **while** Maggie isn't any closer to Kate. If anything, they are further apart.

Theo and Kee are drawn closer together because of the great stress that they are put under. The people who are supposedly helping them – Julian, Luke, Jasper, Syd and others – all end up dead or captured. They have nobody but themselves to rely on. **On the other hand**, Maggie expects her children to help her on her terms: *'there's a few changes coming shortly that might not appeal to you.'* She makes Kate marry against her will, effectively throwing her out of the house. She only cares that Kate is socially accepted again as a married woman. Maggie is not bothered by the fact that all of her children, not just Kate, will be out of the house eventually. She says *'have a good look and see if there are any tears on my face.'* Her family is not any closer together as a result of this journey. They are not drawn closer together in their relationships.

I think Maggie has a very strong and sometimes harsh personality which makes relationships difficult for her. She is a very controlling person. **This is a bit similar** to Theo at the start of the film. He seems to care for nobody but himself. He is a man with little hope in life and he seems miserable. However, his journey to freedom with Kee changes him to a more caring and sympathetic person. He even delivers the baby along the way and takes a bullet to help them escape. They grow together almost like a new family, even if the future of the 'family' on earth is doomed. **This is very different** to *Big Maggie*. Although Maggie does want her family name and reputation to continue, she pushes all of her children, not just Kate, away from her in order to achieve this. I don't think this could be called a total success, **although** Maggie seems content and pleased with herself at the end of the play. She doesn't seem to change the way Theo does.

So in the end, the relationship in *Children of Men* was more successful and a lot happier than the relationship shown in *Big Maggie*.

(458 words)

EXAMINER'S ASSESSMENT

Lots of good comparisons made here; the candidate uses the language of the question and indicates the differences; the point about how characters can change is very good; sentence structure, coherence and language skills are of an excellent standard; well done – a top-grade answer.

MARKS AWARDED

12 + 12 + 12 + 4 = 40/40 (O1 Grade)

Useful phrases

There are certain words and phrases that are useful for the Comparative Study. Examiners are on the lookout for them. Provided they are accurate and relevant, you stand a greater chance of scoring well in this section if you include certain phrases. Try to incorporate the following phrases into your answers.

When looking for similarities:

- 'In both texts...'
- 'Similarly to text A, text B...'
- 'I also noted/found/saw/felt that...'
- 'This also occurs/happens/exists in...'
- 'When we look at text B...'
- 'Text A and B both show/demonstrate/indicate/portray...'
- 'In the same way...'
- 'Once again, we see that...'

When looking for differences:

- 'In contrast...'
- 'Unlike in text A...'
- 'What a difference from...'
- 'This is the reverse of...'
- 'This is the opposite to...'
- 'I found that text B differs...'
- 'While X happens in text A, Y happens in text B...'

Essential words and phrases:

- Unlike
- Like
- Similar
- Different
- Contrastingly
- Too
- Also
- Yet
- But
- Whereas
- On the other hand
- However
- Nevertheless
- Consequently
- As a result
- Therefore

8 Poetry

aims
- To outline the prescribed poetry to be studied and suggest a method for breaking down the list for revision purposes.
- To encourage an understanding of poetic technique.
- To demonstrate the importance of the unseen poem and how it helps with revision generally.

Poetry (17.5%)
Unseen – 5% studied – 12.5%

There are two poetry sections in the exam:

a) Unseen Poem (20 marks – 20 minutes)

b) Studied Poetry (50 marks – 45 minutes)

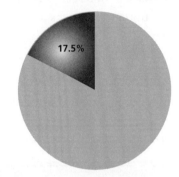

The Vocabulary of Poetry – 'Poetic Terms'

Poetry is a language and style of its own. It is different to other types of writing. Therefore, it is important to be familiar with some terms or techniques that are associated with poetry. Being really familiar with the list on the next page can help improve your written responses. Good answers often include reference to one or other of these terms.

Eavan Boland

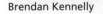

Brendan Kennelly

Sylvia Plath

D. H. Lawrence

The 12 Most Important Poetic Terms!

ALLITERATION – a technique where (usually) the same letter is used repeatedly at the beginning of words in close succession.

> E.g.: *'long, lovely and lush'* (Hopkins in 'Spring') makes the grass seem like it is shooting upwards.

ASSONANCE – the use of similar sounding vowel sounds in poetry, they create a particular sound effect.

> E.g.: *'unintelligible syllables'* (Plath in 'The Arrival of the Bee Box') sounds like the buzzing of a bee hive.

IMAGERY – this is the creation of pictures in the mind of the reader that can have an effect upon the reader's feelings, understandings or reactions. All poetry contains some imagery.

> E.g.: *'a dirty dog, quite comfy'* (Bishop in 'Filling Station'.) is a wonderful picture to imagine on a hot day in rural America.

METAPHOR – a word or phrase to describe something which must not be understood literally. Much poetry is metaphoric because poets aim to describe things in colourful, abstract ways.

> E.g.: *'I am no source of honey'* (Plath in 'The Arrival of the Bee Box') suggests that she might have a darker, inner personality, perhaps one that is suffering.

ONOMATOPOEIA – this involves words which imitate sounds, or where the sound matches closely with the intended meaning.

> E.g.: *'rollrock highroad roaring down'* (Hopkins in 'Inversnaid') brilliantly captures the sound and movement of a waterfall.

PERSONIFICATION – this is to give human characteristics to non-human subjects, or to give life, metaphorically, to sometimes lifeless things.

> E.g.: *'Someone else cut off my head'* – Brendan Kennelly describes himself as an ear of corn that is made into bread in the poem 'Bread'.

PUN – a play on words, which creates a double meaning, sometimes, but not always, for comic effect.

> E.g.: *'The boy <u>saw all</u>'* (Frost, in 'Out, Out—') suggests the boy now understands the real danger he is in, having actually cut his hand with a saw.

SIMILE – this is a description that uses 'as', 'like' or sometimes 'than', to make a comparison between two related subjects. The things being compared may not have an obvious likeness.

> E.g.: *'plain as lettering in the chapels'* (Larkin in 'The Explosion') makes the words the wives hear seem very vivid and clear.

SPEAKER – the **voice** in the poem. **The poet is NOT always the one speaking in the poem,** though often they are the same. 'La Belle Dame Sans Merci' by John Keats is a good example of where more than one voice in the poem is heard and where the voice is not always that of the poet.

STANZA – this is the correct term for a **collection of lines together** in a poem. **Sonnets** have fourteen lines, but can be broken into various 'stanzas' or specific groups of lines. It is a good idea to use this word 'stanza' when answering questions.

THEME – the main idea or issue discussed in a poem. It is not necessarily the subject-matter, but rather the **deeper concern** or **message** that is raised or discussed in the poem.

> E.g.: **'mystery'** is a key theme in Eiléan Ní Chuilleanáin's poem 'Street', even though it describes the movements of a woman working in a butchers.

TONE – associated with feeling or mood, one can imagine the tone of the poem being the sound of the voice that speaks in the poem. It creates a certain mood or 'feeling' to the words.

> E.g.: **Anxiety** and **despair** are the dominant tones in 'Child' by Sylvia Plath.

Answering Questions – Part 1: The Unseen Poem

Unseen Poem (20 MARKS – 20 MINUTES)

- The unseen poem is not too complicated. You will be asked for a reaction to specific issues after some **careful reading**.
- Its purpose is to **test your response to poetry generally** before tackling specific prescribed poetry.
- There are usually **two short questions** asked, both worth 10 marks. There may be a 20-mark question on its own.
- Answers worth 10 marks require about **100 words**. This is about six or seven full sentences as a minimum.
- Answers worth 20 marks require at least two full paragraphs, **up to about 200 words or more**.
- Stick to the '**point–quote–explain**' formula: say something at first, refer and quote from the poem, and explain what you mean.
- It is important to '**move on**' from this question after fifteen minutes. More questions worth more marks are waiting.

Typical questions include:

- **Feelings** generated in the poem;
- **Images** and settings created in the poem;
- **Sounds** heard in the language of the poem;
- **Themes** in the poem: what is the main point being made?
- Your **reaction** to the poem – did you like it? etc.

NOTE: This final point – 'your reaction' – can be a challenging question for 20 marks/15 minutes of work.

If asked for 'your reaction' to the Unseen Poem, refer back to the 'poetic techniques' above:

- Write down what YOU noticed or felt having read the poem.
- Refer to major features like IMAGERY or the THEME of the poem.
- Top-grade answers often explain how the poem makes you 'feel' having read it.
- You are likely to cover some important aspects of the poem in your answer if you follow this advice.

Students that can identify feelings or emotions in the written word typically score well in their answers.

Sample Question 1 – Unseen Poem (20 marks/20 minutes)

Read this poem at least twice and then respond to the questions that follow.

The Scottish poet, Douglas Dunn, writes a poem in which he explores his feelings about a family leaving their home in the city.

A REMOVAL FROM TERRY STREET

On a squeaking cart, they push the usual stuff,
A mattress, bed ends, cups, carpets, chairs,
Four paperback westerns. Two whistling youths
In surplus US Army battle-jackets
Remove their sister's goods. Her husband
Follows, carrying on his shoulders the son
Whose mischief we are glad to see removed,
And pushing, of all things, a lawnmower.
There is no grass in Terry Street. The worms
Come up cracks in concrete yards in moonlight.
That man, I wish him well. I wish him grass.

Douglas Dunn

1. What kind of world is being described in this poem? Refer to the poem in your answer. (10)
2. How, in your opinion, does the writer feel about the family that is leaving Terry Street? Refer to the text of the poem in your answer. (10)

QUESTION 1
SAMPLE ANSWER

> The world of this poem is an urban one, where poverty is apparent. The fact that 'there is no grass on Terry Street' tells me that this must be in a town or city and the poet seems to be laughing at the fact that the family have a lawnmower. The brothers are wearing 'surplus US Army battle-jackets' and pushing a cart with all the family belongings. They are not moving house but instead are being 'removed', as the title says. I think that this may be because they cannot afford the rent or are being re-housed because of anti-social behaviour, perhaps caused by the son who sits on the father's shoulders.
>
> (114 words)

EXAMINER'S ASSESSMENT

This is a really good answer for ten marks. It makes an excellent opening claim that is well supported with five pieces of evidence. The reference to the title is apt and shows that the candidate has read the poem closely.

MARKS AWARDED

6 + 4 = 10/10

QUESTION 2
SAMPLE ANSWER

> I think that the poet has some sympathy for the family. It is contained mostly in the final line. When he says 'I wish him well', I feel that he understands the shame and hardship that is felt if you are thrown out of your house. He sees that the man is doing his best for his family, having a lawnmower that might be used if they get a good new house or make some money if he sells it. He is glad that the son is going, 'whose mischief we are glad to see going', but overall, he does feel a bit sorry for them.
>
> (107 words)

EXAMINER'S ASSESSMENT

This is a really good answer that includes the key word 'sympathy' in the opening sentence. Two quotations are included to back up the claim and the candidate addresses the question with a broad and carefully chosen vocabulary.

MARKS AWARDED

6 + 4 = 10/10
Total for Unseen Poem = 20/20 (O1 Grade)

Sample Question 2 – Unseen Poem (20 marks/20 minutes).

Read the following poem and the two questions on it at least twice before writing your answers.

SEAGULL

We are the dawn marauders.*
We prey on pizza. We kill kebabs.
We mug thrushes for bread crusts
with a snap of our big bent beaks.
We drum the worms from the ground
with the stamp of our wide webbed feet.
We spread out, cover the area –
like cops looking for the body
of a murdered fish-supper.
Here we go with our hooligan yells
loud with gluttony, sharp with starvation.
Here we go bungee-jumping on the wind,
charging from the cold sea of our birth.
This is invasion. This is occupation.
Our flags are black, white and grey.
Our wing-stripes are our rank.
No sun can match the brazen
colour of our mad yellow eyes.

We are the seagulls.
We are the people.

Brian McCabe
*(raiders/robbers)

1. In this poem the poet vividly describes the actions and conduct of seagulls. Choose two of these descriptions which appeal to you most. Explain your choices. **(10)**

2. *We are the seagulls.*
    We are the people.

    From your reading of the poem, what similarities do you think the poet draws between seagulls and humans? Explain your answer. **(10)**

QUESTION 1
SAMPLE ANSWER

I like when he says that the seagulls are like cops looking for a body and when they have mad yellow eyes. The cops are the police so I think he means that the seagulls are like them. People don't like the cops and sometimes seagulls are not liked either. Maybe it's just that they have to do a job when they need to find food they have to kill other animals. Their eyes are mad and yellow and this makes them seem fierce and wicked birds. Overall, it is a really vivid description.

(95 words)

EXAMINER'S ASSESSMENT

The candidate engages with the task and does answer the question asked. Two examples are selected but the candidate would score better with more accurate quotation or by making two distinct points. A 'personal' interpretation of the scene is provided. The language and expression is quite basic but this merits half marks for the effort made.

MARKS AWARDED

3 + 2 = 5/10

QUESTION 2
SAMPLE ANSWER

The seagulls are very like humans the way they kill things and cause trouble for others. 'Here we go with our hooligan yells' is like the way mad football fans riot and cause fights all over the place. I didn't think hooligans were like birds, they are more like wild animals when they get going. I seen many hooligan on the telly but none of them looked like seagulls. But then again, the birds here are described like people so maybe next time I see a seagull, I will think of them as vicious birds that cause trouble for other creatures around them, just like hooligans do.

(108 words)

EXAMINER'S ASSESSMENT

This is an excellent example of a candidate with limited skills really trying to say as much as they can to earn marks. **Crucially, the basic question is answered:** birds are equated with hooligans and the candidate expands upon that idea, with reference to the poem and some personal input. Well done.

MARKS AWARDED

5 + 2 = 7/10

Total = 12/20 (O4 Grade)

key point

You are not asked to 'explain everything' in the unseen poem, but rather to say what the poem means to you.

Answering Questions – Part 2: Prescribed Poetry (50 Marks – 45 minutes)

- Spend about five minutes reading the options and highlighting key words.
- Spend 25 minutes answering the short 10-mark questions and 15 minutes on the longer 20-mark question.
- Total = 45 minutes.
- **FOUR POEMS** from your full list will appear on the page.
- Each year, the exam papers have shown that **TWO** poems come from a combined list studied by everybody doing the exam – Higher or Ordinary Level.
- **TWO** more poems come from a list confined to just Ordinary Level.
- It is important to concentrate on **one list only**.
- **There is no need to revise every poem on the course**.
- This is particularly true if you have been in a class with **mixed Higher/Ordinary** Level students.
- In this book, we will focus on revising just the poems that are found on the combined **Higher/Ordinary** list as most students will have covered these poems.

Choose your poems for revision – don't try to revise them all! Just look at the lists below – you will end up revising about twenty at the very most.

2018 & 2019	
G. M. Hopkins:	Spring
	Inversnaid
E. Ní Chuilleanáin:	Street
	To Niall Woods and Xenya Ostrovskaia, Married in Dublin on 9th September 2009

2018 only	
E. Boland:	Child of Our Time
	This Moment
	Love
P. Durcan:	Wife Who Smashed Television Gets Jail
	Parents
	Sport
R. Frost:	The Tuft of Flowers
	Mending Wall
	Out, Out—
J. Keats:	On First Looking into Chapman's Homer
	La Belle Dame Sans Merci
P. Larkin:	Ambulances
	The Explosion
J. Montague:	The Cage
	The Locket
	Like Dolmens Round My Childhood

2019 only	
E. Bishop:	The Fish
	Filling Station
	The Prodigal
S. Heaney:	A Constable Calls
	The Underground
	A Call
B. Kennelly:	Begin
	Bread
	Saint Brigid's Prayer
D. H. Lawrence:	Baby-Movements II: 'Trailing Clouds'
	Humming-Bird
S. Plath:	Poppies in July
	The Arrival of the Bee Box
	Child
W. B. Yeats:	An Irish Airman Foresees His Death
	The Wild Swans at Coole

How Do I Revise My Prescribed Poetry?

Use the SEE–HEAR–FEEL Approach to Revision

People are instinctively drawn to one of three main reactions to a piece of writing. We are mostly:

1. LOOKERS (visual learners)

OR

2. HEARERS (audio learners)

OR

3. FEELERS (emotional learners)

Of course, we all have eyes, ears and emotions. The point is that we sometimes have **one which is stronger than the other two,** often without realising it. Applied to poetry, this means:

- LOOKER: Yes, I can see the **imagery** of the poem, the colours and shapes, the faces of the people, and the location/setting is clear.

- HEARER: yes, I can hear the beat and rhythm of this poem. I can appreciate the **language** usage. The words sound good to me and I like the way it rhymes (if it does) or the way the poet brings music to the scene.

- FEELER: yes, the poem affected the way I felt. I could feel a certain **tone** – it created a certain mood. It made an impact upon me and I could relate to the experience of the speaker/poet. There was a strong emotional impact within it.

When you put all three together, you should have a sense of what the point of the poem is. You will hopefully grasp the **THEME** of the poem.

key point

> Understanding poetry means identifying the theme – the main issue within – once you have considered the imagery, language and tone.

Question 1: 30 Marks – 25 minutes

Question 1, parts **a**, **b**, and **c**, each worth 10 marks, look for specifics from within the poem. Typical questions asked recently include:

- Specific issues: **content/tone/imagery, etc**.
- **How** does the poet create **image/atmosphere/setting**?
- What do we **learn** from this poem?
- What is your **favourite phrase/line** in the poem?
- Why do you think this poem is so **popular**?
- What **questions are raised** by this poem?
- How would you **feel** if you were... etc.?
- What is the **message** of the poem?
- Describe the **relationship** between... etc.

Have a look at the notes on this prescribed poem and the typical approach to a 10-mark question.

Notes on Prescribed Poems

1. Gerard Manley Hopkins (2018–19)
'Spring'

See	Hear	Feel
Springtime; weeds, wheels, bird's eggs; woodland coming 'alive' and lambs running in the fields; speaker wonders **what causes all this to happen?** remembers the 'Garden of Eden' in the Bible; **a time before sin,** when we were innocent, just like the animals in the fields. **Powerful religious imagery** throughout, calling us to prayer and repentance. Wonderful **sounds** are	throughout this poem, e.g. **assonance** – weeds and wheels; **alliteration** – long, lovely, low; look, little, low; birdsong – 'echoing timber'; rinse and wring'; 'strikes like lightnings'; lambs playing – 'have fair their fling'; **wonder** at this beautiful scene – 'all this juice and joy'.	**Awe** and **amazement** – spring is such an **awe-inspiring** time; the re-awakening of the earth and the **joy of life** itself; the last six lines pose a question: **how can we retain all this wonder and joy before sin clouds our minds?** Speaker feels that it is **Christ that saves us from sin.**

Typical 10-mark question and answer

- This poem appeared on the 2017 exam paper as well as in 2011. Here is an example of a 10-mark question and sample answer to go with it.
- Look at how the grid above – 'see–hear–feel' – can help with answering these types of questions.
- Remember that for 10 marks, you should write at least 6 or 7 sentences in about 8–10 minutes.
- As always: point–quote–explain.

QUESTION

Do you think Hopkins creates a sense of prayer in the last six lines of the poem? Refer to the poem in support of your answer. (10 marks)

SAMPLE ANSWER:

I **agree** that Hopkins **creates a sense of prayer** in the last six lines. This is because the **imagery is mostly religious,** or at least in my mind, it makes me think of **religious themes. (Point)**

Words like **'Christ, lord'** and the mention of **'Maid's child'** indicate the person of Jesus. There is also a mention of the **Garden of Eden**. These images recall our fall from grace and how humans became sinful. **(Quote/Reference)**

This poem therefore is a celebration of all that is beautiful in nature, especially in spring. But we also must pray for our sinfulness in this beautiful world because according to Hopkins, it is 'worth the winning' when Christ saves us. **(Explain)**

(113 words)

EXAMINER'S ASSESSMENT

This answer would receive the full 10 marks as it does exactly what is required from the question.

NOW – apply the same type of approach with the rest of the poems and notes below.

'Inversnaid'

See	Hear	Feel
Speaker finds himself alongside a **small Scottish stream** – a 'darksome burn, horseback brown' that roars down the hillside; froth and bubbles; dark pools; it rolls through steep hillsides (braes) and through boggy ground (heathpack, fern); speaker wonders aloud **what the world would be like without this wet and wild scenery?**	The **power of the river**: darksome, horseback, rollrock, highroad, coop, comb, fleece, foam, flutes, lake falls home; 'fawn-froth' suggests **the slower movement further down**; there is **alliteration** all throughout: 'degged – dappled – dew'; 'flitches of fern'; 'Long live the weeds and the wilderness yet'; **suggests the stream is ongoing, like life itself.**	**Awe** in the face of such raw power and beauty; speaker is **enthralled** by this apparently minor little stream flowing down the hillside; speaker turns to **wonder** what the world would be like without ('bereft of') this wild and beautiful scene; **defiant** at the end, **hoping that this scene will continue forever.**

2. Eiléan Ní Chuilleanáin (2018–19)
'Street'

See	Hear	Feel
A **mysterious scene, unexplained**; an unnamed man sees a butcher's daughter; **mesmerised** by her beauty, seeing her white trousers and dangling knife; **follows her** down a laneway; a half-open door, stairs with her **bloody footprints** leading to the top; **what is about to happen and why?** We don't know.	A simple **narrative poem** – it tells a **story**; the verb 'dangling' is important – the detail is left out there for us; we do not know what is going on or what will happen next; 'shambles' is an old word for the 'slaughterhouse', but also a 'mess' or a 'confusion': We **watch rather than listen** to this scene.	A slightly 'sinister' poem – maybe an **innocent fantasy** of a young man; but the specific details – butcher, knife, love, laneway, door, bloodstains, bare feet – are the **typical details of a murder mystery** or a gothic horror scene; something **uncomfortable** and **odd** about these unexplained events.

'To Niall Woods and Xenya Ostrovskaia, Married in Dublin On 9th September 2009'

See	Hear	Feel
A newly married couple, setting out on a journey, the **metaphor** of 'following a star'; given a **'mother's blessing'**; arriving in a new land, discovering new things but remembering those from the past; part of a 'fairytale'; **things will work out in the end, according to the mother;** just like Ruth, the Moabite woman in the Old Testament.	'Pitching its tent' – a **metaphor** for settling down together; **'You will'** is repeated – the mother is certain about the future; the 'talking cat' is an **image** from folklore, associated with witches, or the **'wise old woman'**; 'trust' is a key word – the speaker asks that they **trust in her wisdom and her blessing.**	**Mild humour** throughout; a **quirky** and **unusual** 'mother's blessing' to a newly married couple; she speaks with wisdom: 'leave behind', you will find, 'you will see', 'you will have to trust me'. The end is **uplifting:** for all the uncertainty about the future and the troubles she faced, things worked out fine for Ruth in the Bible.

3. Eavan Boland (2018)
'Child of Our Time'

See	Hear	Feel
Child being sung to sleep – a 'lullaby' – changes to a **death scene**; baby screaming; **contrasts dramatically** with the gentle, homely imagery of a baby at rest, in bed; **adults wondering** how to react – 'idle talk' has led to the death; cradle has been 'robbed'; baby is now 'asleep' in death; **we must not let this happen again.**	References to **music** contrasts with the subject of a bomb exploding: **'lullaby; song; cry; tune; rhythm; rhymes'**; harsh, blunt language describes the dead child – **'discord; murder; death; dead; broken'.** Numerous **emotive phrases** – 'the discord of your murder', 'robbed your cradle' we 'hear' the **cries of pain and anguish.**	**Tenderness** and **love** are evident at the beginning; but this is destroyed by the sense of **outrage** and **anguish** in stanza 2 – adults 'should have known how' to avoid this needless killing; there is some **hope** in the end – maybe from this death we can 'rebuild' ourselves around this image, to **ensure it won't happen again.**

'This Moment'

See	Hear	Feel
Somewhere in the **'suburbs'** – evening time – and we are **peering in the window of a family home**; stars and moths in the sky; black dark contrasts with the yellow colours inside; a child runs to its mother's arms; **everything happens very quickly** – then the 'moment' passes.	**'Neighbourhood'** suggests a community of neighbours, **friendly and in conversation**; but there is a **'silence'** about this moment; it will also pass very quickly; 'yellow as butter' is a **simile**; even in such silence, many things are happening; perhaps **we don't pay enough attention to these small things**?	**Anticipation** – 'things are getting ready/to happen/out of sight'; **mystery** – what is actually going on? The arrival of darkness makes us **slightly fearful**; but the comforting arms of the mother **reassures us**; 'apples sweeten' suggests a pleasant ending; but fruit can **metaphorically suggest** the loss of innocence.

'Love'

See	Hear	Feel
Speaker addresses her husband; remembering life in midwest America; river represents the journey of their love together; remembering their challenges, how love was fragile: 'feather and muscle of wings'; 'fire and air'; how their child nearly died; now they are older, the speaker sees the husband as a hero; but wonders will their love ever be so intense again?	Bridge, river, water – all suggest a journey or a challenge ahead; references to 'hero' evoke myths and legends – their journey together has been difficult and not without troubles; 'Amish' reference makes it seem very basic, unexciting; now 'we speak plainly' and 'we hear each other clearly' suggest that both are now wiser and more understanding.	Sombre, serious tone at the beginning – remembering the past but in a 'matter-of-fact' way; calm, reflective tones in stanzas 2–4; changes in stanza 5 to a longing for a return to more 'romantic' times – 'blazing', 'gilded' and 'epic' call for a more intense, exciting relationship; a sense of uncertainty at the end – never the same again?

4. Paul Durcan (2018)
'Wife Who Smashed Television Gets Jail'

See	Hear	Feel
Courtroom scene, but something comical about it all; lines 1–21: the 'evidence' of the husband; lots of ludicrous details, e.g. 'took off her boots and smashed in the television'; 'mother has a fondness for *Kojak*'; lines 22–26: the Judge pronounces his verdict – again with ludicrous detail: 'television... a basic unit of the family'; 'leave to appeal was refused.'	Ranting, agitated husband and father delivering his evidence; attempts to be formal: 'My Lord'; violent actions are indicated: 'smashed; marched; boot through the screen; snarled;' the judgement is delivered in formal tones but with a comical edge – 'Jail is the only place for them'.	Disturbing detail on the surface; this is a reversal of the more likely scene – it is discomforting to have a mother, rather than a father, doing this to her family; a strange mix between tragedy and comedy – a sense of drama and conflict mixed with the bizarre details of the case; ultimately, a comical poem, poking fun at the sensitive topic of domestic violence.

'Parents'

See	Hear	Feel
A child's face – the word 'drowned' and the repetition of 'sea' makes this a frightening image; metaphorically, the child is 'in danger'; 'locked out of their own home' suggests a distance or a great danger in the parent–child relationship; 'fearful fish' and 'calling out to them' continue the frightening imagery; parents left 'stranded', staring at their 'lost child'.	'Sea' and 'See' (pun) are both used – the 'sea' of sleep? or the 'sea' of confusion? 'locked out' – a very harsh sounding phrase; child calling out in the night; parents cannot hear nor respond; a very distressing sound; 'inside' versus 'outside' and repetition of 'drowned' suggests the sound of panic and desperation on the part of the parents.	Distressing and disturbing; a sense of distance and disconnection between parents and child; 'mouths open' create the sense that the parents are in shock or in panic; 'they cannot hear'; 'they are outside the sea'; 'they stare at the drowned, drowned face'; a genuinely downbeat and 'depressing' tone throughout.

'Sport'

See	Hear	Feel
Father hoping the son will succeed at sport; son is in a **psychiatric hospital** but plays a game of football, as **goalkeeper**; father spectates; various **vulnerable and disturbed characters play on the team**; son plays really well: 'I did not flinch in the goals'; son had **tried incredibly hard to please the father**; he never managed to do so again after this event.	**Narrative language** – 'I was selected to play for Grangegorman Mental Hospital'; very **colourful and varied characters** play on both teams – 'gapped teeth, red faces, oily frizzy hair, bushy eyebrows... cases of schizophrenia'; **father finally praises his son** as he sniffs his approval: '**Well played, son**'.	**Reflective** – speaker remembers the '**one time**' father praised him; **fearful** that he would 'let him down'; **pride** that he played so well; **mixed feelings now** on reflection – he seldom if ever rose to these heights again.

5. Robert Frost (2018)
'The Tuft of Flowers'

See	Hear	Feel
Rural or 'pastoral' scene, speaker is **alone**, ready to turn the freshly mown grass; **mysterious 'other' figure** cut it yesterday; butterfly also notices the scene; a small tuft remains uncut amid the mown grass; the speaker feels a 'spirit kindred' with the other worker, who 'spared' this tuft; **they share the same views and opinions, even though they don't know each other.**	**Beautifully crafted phrases**: 'isle of trees'; 'whetstone' (used to sharpen the blade); 'bewildered butterfly'; 'tremulous wing'; 'tall tuft of flowers'; 'leaping tongue of bloom'; 'reedy brook'; 'the scythe had spared'; 'I worked no more alone'; 'held brotherly speech'; 'Men work together'.	**Loneliness**; lacking any enthusiasm; changes to **delight** when the butterfly shows him the tuft of flowers; **spirit is uplifted** with this 'message from the dawn'; **relaxed and contented** at the end – the flowers are a **sign of life and the presence of another**, similar-minded person.

'Mending Wall'

See	Hear	Feel
Rural scene; a wall is being repaired by the speaker and his neighbour; they speak to each other; **it is like a game, but not quite friendly**; it seems quite **normal and routine**, but holding the stones, the neighbour looks like a 'savage'; they agree that '**good fences make good neighbours**'.	'Frozen-ground-swell': some **invisible force makes the wall fall down**; 'we meet to walk the line'; 'we wear our fingers rough'; 'Why do they make good neighbours?'; the neighbour 'moves in darkness as it seems to me'; 'walling in or walling out?'; 'Like an old stone savage armed'; **lots of questioning phrases**.	**Friendly banter**; sense of 'purpose' and good relationships; leads to **curiosity and uncertainty**; speaker is **not entirely pleased** – why the need for walls? Why not live and let live? Speaker **accepts that the neighbour will not change** – the wall will remain; life goes on as before.

'Out, Out—'

See	Hear	Feel
Rural Vermont; young boy working hard sawing timber; evening time; work nearly done; boy cuts his hand very badly; panic; sister is with him; doctor tries to save him but it's too late; he dies; the other people don't seem too bothered; life 'carries on' as they 'turned to their affairs'.	Sharp, clear sounds of the work being done: 'buzz-saw' 'snarled and rattled'; 'stove-length sticks of wood'; 'sunset'; 'supper'; 'But the hand!'; 'a rueful laugh'; 'the boy saw all' – a great pun; 'big boy doing a man's work'; 'the watcher at his pulse took fright'; 'little–less–nothing' and 'they' don't seem to care too much.	Pride – 'hard work' is what makes a boy into a man; anticipation of supper; replaced by shock – the saw 'leaped out of the boy's hand'; a 'rueful laugh' suggests a near-comic moment, but instead panic ensues: 'don't let them sister!'; a sense of great distress takes hold – he 'puffs his lips out' in pain; but there is no real grief as he dies – life is cold, short and brutal.

6. John Keats (2018)
'On First Looking into Chapman's Homer'

See	Hear	Feel
Speaker reflecting upon his 'travels' in the world of books and learning, not a physical journey as such; compares himself to an astronomer ('watcher of the skies') or an explorer ('Cortez... with eagle eyes'); and is thankful to the writer 'Chapman' for translating the work of Homer, from Greek.	A beautiful, rhythmic sonnet: fourteen lines that have a specific rhyme and rhythm; heavily metaphoric words are used throughout: 'realms of gold', 'goodly states', 'kingdoms', 'western islands' all refer to books he has read; 'deep-brow'd Homer' indicates intelligence; 'ken' means vision or awareness; 'stout' means brave or strong.	Reflective and descriptive in the octet (first eight lines); speaks of his loyalty ('fealty') to learning and his gratitude/thanks to 'Chapman'; switches to excitement and enthusiasm in the sestet (last six lines) as he feels like a great explorer discovering the wonders of the world.

'La Belle Dame Sans Merci'

See	Hear	Feel
An unnamed narrator asks a knight what is wrong with him; he tells the story of meeting a beautiful lady – 'a faery's child' – they fell in love and they made 'sweet moan'. They go to her 'elfin grot', he kisses her (stanza 8) but he falls asleep; on awakening, she is gone; so he is left alone and 'palely loitering' as indicated at the start.	'La Belle Dame' is the beautiful lady; 'Sans Merci' means that she is 'without pity'; 'O what can ail thee' – the language of a literary ballad; other examples: thy brow; woe-begone; fast withereth; I love thee true; death-pale were they all; regular four-line stanzas – the fourth line is shorter and summarises each stanza.	Curiosity: what is wrong with this knight? Intrigue: who is this mysterious lady? Where did she come from? Excitement: they head to her cave and the kiss each other – but what happened then? Great disappointment: the loss of his lady also means that his appearance fades; love brings death and decay rather than happiness.

7. Philip Larkin (2018)
'Ambulances'

See	Hear	Feel
The journeys made by an ambulance every day; locked doors on the back look like a confession box; speeding through a city; stopping at accidents; red and white colours – blood and bandages; injured people are loaded up; taken away from loved ones; cars move aside to let the ambulance pass.	Siren wailing during the day: 'loud noons of cities'; children playing, people shouting, all stops as the injured person is loaded up: '"poor soul" they whisper at their own distress'; the 'sudden shut of loss' as the door closes; 'brings closer what is left to come' makes us think about our own 'end' one day.	Sombre, serious tone – the ambulance goes about its business; 'wild white face' creates a sense of shock; pause for reflection; 'deadened air' has a foreboding* tone to it; respectful behaviour from the traffic; we 'dull to distance' our own feelings as we try to put the scene out of our minds. *a sense that something frightening is just ahead

'The Explosion'

See	Hear	Feel
Coalmine; middle of the day; sunshine causes shadows on the slagheap; hard-edged miners chatting; one miner chases rabbits and finds birds' eggs; laughter and pipe-smoking; a tremor occurs – cows stop chewing; sun dims; something awful has happened; images of the dead float before us; they walk towards the sun, one miner carrying the same eggs as before; an image of rebirth and a new start.	Alliteration: 'In the sun the slagheap slept'; nothing seems out of place, a quiet day at work; 'oath-edged talk' – the colourful language of the workers; 'freshened silence' makes the explosion even more noticeable; 'Fathers, brothers, nicknames, laughter'; stanza 6 is sombre, religious in tone, like a sermon. We hear the prayers of the wives and families.	'Shadows' suggests something unseen, frightening maybe? 'Through the tall gates' hints at the gates of heaven; is something about to happen; a sense of conviction* once the dead have been buried: 'We shall see them face to face—' Shock and anguish turns to hope: the miners are now 'walking... towards them'. *the state of being 'completely convinced'

8. John Montague (2018)

'The Cage'

See	Hear	Feel
Speaker's father: the 'least happy man I know;' a **tragic image of a sad life**, working in New York's subway selling tickets; alcoholic who drank to 'brute oblivion;' but a man who worked every day; was **friendly to his neighbours**; he returns to Ireland when older but **the relationship is no better**; the speaker then must leave himself; **sees many people like his father working in the subway**.	'Least happy' – **a blunt start**; 'pallor' – poor complexion, lacking colour; 'shudder' – an uncomfortable feeling; neat whiskey – 'strong' alcohol; 'extending his smile... belled by St Teresa's Church'; **outwardly he is a jolly individual it seems**; 'ghostly forehead' sounds like **his souls still lives in the underground somewhere**, many years later.	**Painful memories**; but 'traditional Irishman' hints at **pride; sympathy** for the father – he only feels 'at home' when he drinks neat whiskey; **no great fondness*** back in Ireland – 'we did not smile in the shared complicity of a dream'; a sense of **loss and personal grief** – the memory of the father lives on: 'I see his bald head behind the bars of the small booth'. ***the state of great 'affection' or attraction**

'The Locket'

See	Hear	Feel
Mother dies; speaker writes a **'lament'*** for her passing; his own birth was very difficult for her; mother wanted a girl; lack of money in the home; child was given away to be reared elsewhere; child visits the mother but she tries not to get 'too fond' of him; 'harsh logic' of a 'forlorn woman' in a difficult situation; the **'mysterious blessing'** – mother always had a locket with his picture in it round her neck – he never knew until she died. *a poem or prayer written to mourn a dead person	**Very painful childbirth**; 'fertile source of guilt and pain'; 'double blunder'; the wrong sex and wrong way around; **father singing songs while drunk**; 'love flies up the chimney'; 'court you like a young man' – the child wants to be with his mother; 'wound into your cocoon of pain' – **the emotional suffering of the mother**; 'forlorn' woman – **she is all alone, troubled**; 'always around your neck' – but she **never forgot her son**.	Mixture of **celebration and lament** – some painfully true details from life are remembered; **tenderness of the mother** (infant curls of brown) contrasts the harsh reality ('don't come again'); **innocence and playfulness of the young speaker**; memory of the beautiful young woman, the 'belle of your small town'; a sense of **deep love and pure devotion** in the final stanza: his mother always wore him close to her heart.

'Like Dolmens Round my Childhood'

See	Hear	Feel
Various elderly people all living in rural isolation*; all with their specific traits and appearances; **each of them dies eventually** – 'sometimes they were found by neighbours, silent keepers of a smokeless hearth'; **the speaker once feared these people** – they 'trespassed on his dreams' – but **they are an important part of the country and the story of who we are**; they 'live on' as he feels their 'shadows pass' over him one day. *apart and alone, away from all others	Jamie McCrystal, a kind soul, singing to himself; Maggie Owens, a local 'witch' with her various animals, **complaining** (lonely need to 'deride') about everybody; the 'Nialls,' a family of blind people, who **use the wireless radio** all the time; Mary Moore, a fierce woman who **reads love stories to herself**; Wild Billy Eagleson, **proudly marching with the Orange Order**, even though he is 'forsaken by both creeds'; (Nationalist and Unionist). **The speaker can hear their dead voices from beyond the grave.**	Stanzas 1–5: each contains a mix of **description and a kind-hearted reflection** on why the people are the way they are; the speaker seeks to understand these people; he is **critical of his younger self** who saw these people as 'gaunt figures of fear and friendliness'; he is **respectful of them now** as they have moved into the 'dark permanence of ancient forms'; they are part of local folklore for the rest of time.

9. Elizabeth Bishop (2019)
'The Fish'

See	Hear	Feel
Fishing on a lake; fish with beautiful colours; big eyes; brown gills; green weeds; **five hooks still stuck in his jaw (important image)**; rainbow-coloured oil in the water; rusted orange; frightened look; **speaker lets the fish go free.**	'Tremendous fish'; 'grunting weight'; 'full-blown roses'; 'like medals with their ribbons' (simile); 'a five-haired beard of wisdom' (metaphor); 'I let the fish go' (narrative poem).	**Excitement** at first; but the speaker then describes the scene as if from a distance; **admiration** for the fish; changes to **sympathy** near the end – the speaker sees how **the fish has already suffered** but has overcome previous hardships and survived; so she lets him go.

'Filling Station'

See	Hear	Feel
Small rural filling station; dirty with **oil and grease everywhere**; a dog sits on a wicker sofa; the owner and his sons appear; **small glimpses of colour** – comics, a begonia flower, a doily (napkin), oil cans ('Esso').	'Oh but it is dirty'; 'Be careful with that match!'; 'several saucy greasy sons assist' **(alliteration)**; 'dirty dog, quite comfy' **(imagery)**; 'Why? Why? Why, oh why?'; 'Somebody' is repeated – **hints at an absent figure, probably a mother.**	**Startling** beginning; **disgust** at first; **mocking** the dirtiness of it all; leads to **curiosity** and **intrigue**: what is this place? The importance of 'home', regardless of what it looks like, is hinted at. Concludes with **mystery**: who is the 'somebody'?

'The Prodigal'

See	Hear	Feel
Rotten pig-sty; **filth everywhere**; pigs watching the young man; he tries to bond with them; he has an alcohol problem; **sunrise suggests a new start**; but he remains 'exiled*'; farmer has little sympathy; pigs seem happy; he dreams of returning home someday, but not. yet. *the state of being barred from entering one's home land; a punishment of some sort	'Prodigal' – a wasteful person; 'brown enormous odor' (pigs); 'plastered' (pun on drunkenness); 'sickening' for the man to live like this; 'the first star' – an image of fear as the darkness comes; 'Ark' – like Noah's ark, a safe place for the time being; 'shuddering insights' suggest the internal pain for the man.	**Disgust; dread; alienation; desperation** – especially to be accepted by anyone, even the pigs; a glint of **hope** each morning; replaced by a **fear of failure** with the arrival of evening; **powerlessness** – 'beyond his control'; **guilt**; concludes with a decision, an **assertiveness** – 'finally... to go home'.

10. Seamus Heaney (2019)
'A Constable Calls'

See	Hear	Feel
Local RUC Policeman visits the young speaker's home; bike and clothing described very closely; father makes his 'tillage returns' and **the policeman takes note**; a very 'officious' man; 'arithmetic and fear'; belt, baton case, polished holster and Domesday Book complete the **imposing picture**; speaker wonders if his father is being honest; he imagines the 'black hole' of a police cell; the constable leaves and **his bike 'ticks' away into the distance.**	'Mud-splasher', 'rubber cowl', 'fat black handle-grips', 'spud', 'dynamo', 'pedals', 'boot of the law' – **all communicate a big, awkward, uncomfortable presence**; 'pressure'; 'sweating'; 'heavy ledger'; bicycle; 'tick, tick, tick' is just like a bomb ready to explode.	'His' bicycle – he isn't referred to by his title – there is an **awkward discomfort at his presence**; **fascination** of the young speaker; turns to **fear as he thinks of the barracks**; there is a '**menacing**' tone as he cycles away – he will be back some day...

'The Underground'

See	Hear	Feel
Man and woman rushing to a concert; he is behind her as her buttons fall off in the rush; going 'underground' on the London Tube, they are late – it is **like a journey into the unknown, like their new marriage**; this is their honeymoon; one is leading the other but also one chases the other; 'damned if I look back' suggests **there is only one way to go from here – forwards**.	'Vaulted tunnel' – a journey into the deep; 'like a fleet god gaining on you' – **speaker enjoys the pursuit as a young lover**; 'moonlighting' suggests that they are involved in secretive or illegal activities by night; 'all attention for your step' – **the speaker realises that they are now together in all things**; they must look out for each other, like Hansel and Gretel.	**Tension, excitement and anxiety** all rolled into one in the first two stanzas; journeying through dark, crowded tunnels, racing to the theatre, but also anxious not to lose each other; **calm is restored near the end** but the speaker is still **anxious as to what their future together holds** – 'bared and tensed as I am'.

'A Call'

See	Hear	Feel
Speaker calling his elderly parents by phone; the mother goes to get the father from the garden; he is weeding; **very careful and meticulous*** – 'touching, inspecting, separating' – the speaker has time to wait and **listen to the clock ticking in the background** – like a clock ticking down to death; **realising our mortality, he almost says he loves his father when he does eventually speak.** *****very close attention to detail**	'"Hold on" she said' – contrasts with the clock ticking later – **time doesn't wait for anyone**; 'rueful' is an important word – both father and son share something of 'regret' in common – father regrets killing weeds, son regrets not having a more open relationship with him; the **irony*** here – the phone call is **mostly filled with silent thoughts and background noise.** *****a contradiction between what is expected and what actually happens**	**Uplifting, positive, everyday conversation between mother and son**; admiration for the father's **dedication and hard-working attitude**; but great **tension: to share his feelings or hold back?** 'I nearly said I loved him' carries the main message of the poem: **we only have a short time on earth in which to express our love.**

11. Brendan Kennelly (2019)
'Begin'

See	Hear	Feel
Starting a new day: 'sight of the light at the window'; traffic building up, **springtime**, flowers growing, bridges from one place to another, young girls dressed up, people dying but they are 'with us still'; **couples enjoying each other's company**; even if there are troubles all around us (we live in a world that dreams of ending); **we must always continue and try to 'begin' again**.	'Summoning' birds – they call us to wake up; **typical sounds of a morning in the city**; (Pembroke Road in Dublin for example;) roar of morning traffic; rain falling; seagulls foraging; couples chatting quietly together as the world passes by. The **'arrogant loneliness'** of the swans is interesting – they silently float by, but are they happy?	Lines 1–12: an **energetic** and **enthusiastic** start to the poem; **encouraging** us to embrace the new day; Lines 13–24 are more **cautious and slightly anxious**: 'loneliness', 'end', 'unknown', 'sudden rain', 'stark', 'dreams of ending', 'about to give in' all hint at the close possibility of disaster at any moment; hence the call to **embrace life now, in this moment**.

'Bread'

See	Hear	Feel
Corn being cut – but the corn speaks as if alive, excellent example of **personification**; moulded and kneaded into dough by a woman (the speaker's mother and grandmother come to mind); he is 'shaped with skill'; he brings 'comfort' to her even when she uses a knife to cut him; put in an oven to cook; **gives thanks for life that was given to him**; ultimately it affirms **the life-giving power of all women**.	'Someone else' – the **violence of the harvest is not important**; what follows is a sensual description of being shaped and moulded by a woman's hands; **very suggestive words**: 'delicate', 'kiss', 'lying down', 'fine', 'legendary', 'shapes me with her skill', 'slits', 'stabs', 'perfection', 'dream', **'I come to life at her finger ends'**.	Initially **frightening** – 'cut off my head' – but giving way to a sense of **love, intimacy and togetherness**; the woman shapes him into what he is and he is 'all that can happen to men' – he is her creation.

'St Brigid's Prayer'

See	Hear	Feel
St Brigid speaking; she offers God a 'lake of beer'; the poem is **her desire to reward those who suffer on earth with a reward in heaven** – she would give 'cups of love' and 'sweet pitchers of mercy' to all those in heaven; God, Jesus, the Three Marys and everybody else would **all share a beer together in heaven.**	'Heavenly Host' – a **pun** on 'host', like at a party; 'tippling' gives it an informal sense; a 'heart and a half' – Brigid will do this with **great enthusiasm;** the 'happy heart is true' and 'make men contented for their own sake' suggests that **we should celebrate for celebration's sake,** not to be suffering always; 'special welcome to the women'; 'every drop would be a prayer' – a **metaphor** for celebration.	An unusual and slightly **'irreverent'* tone;** but it is essentially a poem about **kindness, celebration and seeking happiness;** there is enough suffering in the name of religion; 'I'd make heaven a cheerful spot' **contrasts more sombre and serious images of the Christian afterlife.** ***mildly disrespectful, mocking, playful**

12. D. H. Lawrence (2019)
'Baby-Movements II: "Trailing Clouds"'

See	Hear	Feel
Lines 1–7 – the baby is described like a **honey-bee, clinging to a flower;** clinging to the speaker – most likely the poet himself, speaking as if he is a 'mother'. Lines 8–10 – the baby is a 'burden' that **depends entirely on the mother for life.** Lines 11–16 – the baby now seems quite heavy, as if **mother and baby are weighed down by some 'weariness'.**	'drenched, drowned bee'; 'numb and heavy'; 'laid laughterless on her cheek'; even though the scene is **silent,** we can sense **some great upheaval has occurred;** 'sways... like sorrowful, storm-heavy boughs... storm bruised young leaves'; **heaviness and weariness suggest a great strain** in being the parent of this child.	Tremendous sense of **connection and dependency** all through; love is also very much evident as the child 'So clings to me' and also 'swings to my lullaby'; 'burden' and 'downwards' are two key words that suggest the feeling of being **overwhelmed by the challenges of being a parent;** weariness also suggests how tiring and demanding this role is.

'Humming-Bird'

See	Hear	Feel
Speaker imagines a time long ago; the hummingbird survived down through all the centuries through its **fierce determination** – 'went whizzing through the slow, vast, succulent stems'; it 'flashed ahead of creation,' surviving despite its small size and lack of flowers to provide nectar; maybe **we have underestimated a creature like the humming-bird**, looking through 'the wrong end of the telescope of Time'.	'Primeval-dumb' – **a time before history, long ago**; the humming-bird 'raced down avenues' while everything else moved so slowly; the 'heave' of matter is so slow, while the 'whizzing' bird flies onwards; 'jabbing, terrifying monster'; the humming-bird **sounds like a giant dinosaur**; 'Luckily for us': the speaker remarks that humans are lucky that his imaginative story is not true.	**Light-hearted descriptions**; not to be taken literally; reflective **imaginative thoughts** by the speaker; 'I believe' is not a scientific fact but just an imaginative thought; **humorous ending** – 'luckily for us' the humming-bird is small and harmless.

13. Sylvia Plath (2019)
'Poppies in July'

See	Hear	Feel
A field of poppies; images of **hell**; flickering flames; a hand in the fire; a mouth that is bleeding; red skirts; 'opiates' – the mind-altering substances in drugs; **images of sickness**: 'nausea' and suffering ('marry a hurt like that'); a glass jar or container, holding this 'poison' that **makes the speaker dull and lifeless**.	'Little' – suggests **something delicate or harmless but NOT in this case**; 'it exhausts me' – the speaker sounds **worn out, anxious, depressed maybe?**; 'a mouth just bloodied' – domestic violence maybe?; 'If I could bleed or sleep!' – **a strange question; perhaps looking for a relief from some great anxiety**; 'dulling', 'stilling', 'colourless': all these words indicate **a numbness and a longing for release**, perhaps from life itself.	Initially **curious**; lots of questions; wondering about the power of the poppies; **intrigued** by their unusual properties; 'A mouth just bloodied:' a change in direction – **much more violent suggestions**; **anxious questions** in stanza 5 – leads to desperate pleading in stanza 6; a **disturbing and frightening conclusion** with the word 'colourless' – there is **no energy or enthusiasm left** in the speaker; she is deflated.

'The Arrival of the Bee Box'

See	Hear	Feel
A bee hive arrives for the speaker; **grotesque* and disturbing imagery is used:** 'coffin of a midget'; 'square baby'; locked, no windows; bees are making a serious racket; **compared to African slaves on ships;** speaker feels like Emperor Caesar, given the **power** she has over them; speaker continues to **wonder about them;** decides to set them free tomorrow... **but will it happen?** *horrible and disgusting	**Brilliant poetic technique,** especially the use of sound e.g. **assonance** ('square baby'/'din in it'/'blond colonnades'); **onomatopoeia** ('angrily clambering'/ 'unintelligible syllables'); the effect is to create the sound of a beehive that contains thousands of bees; speaker is engrossed in them – **mentions 'I' eighteen times;** the speaker is involved in an **'internal monologue' speaking to herself** – she is **metaphorically** 'no source of honey'; she sounds **doubtful.**	**Uncertainty,** leading to many questions; the speaker must decide what to do and this is a dilemma; the 'power' she has over them ('I am the owner') does not rest easily with her; she **'wonders'** how hungry they are; wonders would they just ignore her and fly away?; 'funeral veil' is an ominous image – does the speaker look forward to her own death? It is unclear what is 'temporary' – the bees/box/speaker herself? **There is no absolute answer.**

'Child'

See	Hear	Feel
Newborn baby; clear-eyed and innocent; colours and experiences from **early childhood;** flowers and animals; but things **change with the word 'Pool';** the 'darkness' it hints at is **frightening;** 'troublous wringing of hands' is a **famous image of anxiety and deep distress;** the 'ceiling without a star' is a **life for the baby without its mother.**	'Clear eye'; 'absolutely beautiful thing'; 'colour and ducks'; 'zoo of the new'; all combine to capture brilliantly the **sounds of a wonderfully happy new mother and child;** 'Little' – the word is placed on its own; **the child is vulnerable, on many levels;** 'troublous wringing of hands' – things change dramatically; **mother is very anxious, and despairing.**	**Pride; pure love and adoration;** the speaker wants the child to only have pleasant experiences; **excitement** at the possibilities to come – the 'zoo of the new'; **great ambition** for the child – 'grand and classical' images; but the final stanza is **shocking and heart-breaking in its honesty** – the speaker committed suicide two weeks later.

14. W. B. Yeats (2019)
'An Irish Airman Foresees His Death'

See	Hear	Feel
Irish Soldier; flying his plane for the British Army in the First World War; **he is not attached to either side;** he is loyal to his 'people' in the West of Ireland; **his likely death won't matter too much in the end;** he is **happy to be in the air** because it was **his choice;** he considered all things before taking this role; **he is 'balanced' in his thinking** but also in his working and fighting.	The poem is about 'balance' in life, be it in working life or in one's thoughts and attitudes; **the lines of the poem are also balanced, with regular syllables and a perfect rhyming scheme;** 'I know' – the poet is **assured and certain of his position in life;** 'Those' – he seems 'detached' from the two sides in war; 'years to come/years behind', 'life/death', **bring balance to the final lines.**	**Assured confidence;** lack of real commitment to any 'cause'; the speaker does however have a **deep personal feeling or 'impulse of delight' to fly above it all,** to get away from the boring life below, to view the world with a **detached eye from above;** he has **great confidence in his own ability** and is not forced to do this by 'public men nor cheering crowds'.

'The Wild Swans at Coole'

See	Hear	Feel
Autumn; a time of change; speaker goes for a walk nineteen years on from his first visit here and notices fifty-nine swans; he **reflects upon how life has changed since then;** his 'heart is sore' at this point, while they travel along 'unwearied still, lover by lover'; they **remain mysterious and beautiful;** and even if they fly away, they will **delight some other man somewhere else.**	Autumn beauty; a still sky; **clamorous ('noisy') wings above his head;** these swans 'wander where they will' and seem perfectly content; they are 'brilliant creatures'; 'they drift on the still water'; 'mysterious, beautiful'; **the descriptive words and sounds throughout are all positive and uplifting.**	Unclear exactly how the speaker is feeling here – **'mixed emotions';** the positive descriptions of the swans suggest that **he admires them still;** perhaps he is **envious** – they travel 'lover-by-lover' together; maybe he **feels like the 'odd-one-out' of the fifty-nine;** he acknowledges that they will fly away eventually at the end – but he is **confident** that they will 'delight men's eyes' wherever they go.

Sample Questions and Answers – Prescribed Poetry

NOTE: Take a look at the final 'grid' above – it is for Yeats's poem 'The Wild Swans at Coole'. By using the notes in the three boxes, you will find that you have the **raw material** to start your answers. This material is very useful when you cannot predict exactly what the question will be – **so pay attention to the grid for each poem that you choose to revise.**

THE WILD SWANS AT COOLE

The trees are in their autumn beauty,
The woodland paths are dry,
Under the October twilight the water
Mirrors a still sky;
Upon the brimming water among the stones
Are nine-and-fifty swans.

The nineteenth autumn has come upon me
Since I first made my count;
I saw, before I had well finished,
All suddenly mount
And scatter wheeling in great broken rings
Upon their clamorous wings.

I have looked upon those brilliant creatures,
And now my heart is sore.
All's changed since I, hearing at twilight,
The first time on this shore,
The bell-beat of their wings above my head,
Trod with a lighter tread.

Unwearied still, lover by lover,
They paddle in the cold
Companionable streams or climb the air;
Their hearts have not grown old;
Passion or conquest, wander where they will,
Attend upon them still.

But now they drift on the still water,
Mysterious, beautiful;
Among what rushes will they build,
By what lake's edge or pool
Delight men's eyes when I awake some day
To find they have flown away?

W. B. Yeats

SAMPLE QUESTIONS

(a) According to Yeats, what qualities do the swans at Coole Park possess?
Explain your answer.

(10)

(b) Which is your favourite stanza in this poem? Explain why you like it.

(10)

(c) This poem presents many pictures (images) to the reader. Choose two which appeal to you and explain why you find them appealing.
[You may not choose images from the same stanza that you wrote about in 1(b) above]   **(10)**

SAMPLE ANSWER (A):

The swans are described as **mysterious and beautiful**. It is interesting to see that they are not described very well until the last stanza. All through, the poet lets us imagine what they might be like and then uses these words at the end. It **sounds like he has been here before** as he says 'the nineteenth autumn has come upon me/since I first made my count'. The poet has seen the swans many times and now still finds them as mysterious as they were when he first saw them. He also uses the word **'brilliant'** to describe them. This is an excellent word to describe their white colour and he is amazed that even though they are older, their hearts remain the same, 'unwearied' by the passage of time. They are also mysterious because he cannot see what is beneath the water or know what is going through their minds at this time.

(155 words)

EXAMINER'S ASSESSMENT

This is an excellent response and the **question is addressed** immediately in the first sentence with the keywords 'mysterious' and 'beautiful'. Appropriate use of **quotation** throughout and there is **lots of detail** for ten marks. There is clarity in what this candidate is saying since the sentence structures and vocabulary are of a very good standard.

MARKS AWARDED

6 + 4 = 10/10

SAMPLE ANSWER (B):

I really like the fourth stanza. There is personification here because the swans are portrayed as **lovers who spend all their time together**, both in and out of the water. The words 'lover by lover' creates a **great image** of the swans swimming two by two on the lake. This happens in real life since swans mate for life. Maybe the **speaker wishes he could be as the swans are**, together with each other for life. I think it is a wonderful image to have in your mind. Yeats creates a very romantic picture here, although it contrasts with the words 'cold' and 'old', which is maybe how he feels himself, since Maud Gonne refused his proposals more than once. Overall, this stanza is very appealing.

(126 words)

EXAMINER'S ASSESSMENT

A very good answer, making the connection between the plight of the speaker and the predicament of the swans. Appropriate quotation is used and the contrast mentioned near the end is interesting. The vocabulary and expression is of a very good standard.

MARKS AWARDED

6 + 4 = 10/10

SAMPLE ANSWER (C):

The first **image** I like is when the poet says '**now my heart is sore**'. He is in some sort of pain, prompted by the picture of the happy swans, swimming together in pairs. There are fifty-nine so this suggests that maybe **one swan is lonely and the poet has a connection to that swan**. Yeats more than likely is remembering the time when Maud Gonne rejected his proposal so the image of his heart being sore is very appropriate at this time. I also like the image of the swans that 'have flown away' right at the end. It reminds me of when something close to you dies or passes on and in this case the swans move to their winter home. It is an image of how **things always change and how nothing in nature is always the same**. This is the theme in this poem, which is that everything changes in nature even if our love for others is eternal.

(161 words)

EXAMINER'S ASSESSMENT

The candidate has provided two images from the relevant stanzas and has addressed the question is a precise way. There is an excellent flow to the answer – each sentence builds on the next and the expression is straightforward and well-phrased. The candidate makes a link between the chosen image and the main concerns of the poem, which is noteworthy. This is an excellent answer.

MARKS AWARDED

6 + 4 = 10/10
Total = 30/30 (O1 Grade)

Question 2: 20 Marks – 15 minutes

Question 2, worth 20 marks, is a little different.

- You may be asked to state what you liked/disliked about the entire poem.
- You may be required to use the poem as an inspiration to create an imaginative response.

- You may be asked to go beyond the words of the poem and create your own situation.

For example, you could be asked to write one of these:

- **Letter to the poet;**
- **Diary of one of the characters;**
- **Describe a film based on the poem;**
- **Would you like to be in this place/situation?**
- **What would appeal to/annoy you most about this poem?**
- **Continue the story outlined in the poem.**

NOTE: In recent years, students have had **three options** on this question, so as usual, read all options carefully and make a sound decision.

Sample Questions

2. Answer ONE of the following: [Each part carries 20 marks]
   (i) Based on this poem write an article for a travel magazine in which you encourage tourists to visit Coole Park.

OR

   (ii) *I have looked upon those brilliant creatures,*
   And now my heart is sore.
   From your reading of the poem, explain why the poet feels like this.

OR

   (iii) There is another poem by W. B. Yeats on your course, 'An Irish Airman Foresees His Death'. Which of these two poems appeals to you more? Give reasons for your answer.

SAMPLE ANSWER (III):

> I liked both of the Yeats poems on the course. If I was to choose one it would be 'An Irish Airman Foresees His Death'. I have two reasons. First, the airman comes across as a much happier speaker than the man at Coole Park. Even though he is way above the clouds and on a mission to drop bombs on the enemy, the airman is still calm and balanced, just like the plane he flies. He is ready to do his duty but he does not hate those he kills, nor love those he is supposed to be 'guarding'. Instead, he is there because he is drawn to the excitement and bravery required to do this. He is also pretty sure that he will die – 'I know that I shall meet my fate' – and this does not stop him from carrying out his mission. I admire the airman because he can see a world beyond the war and a life beyond death. Even though war is a terrible thing

and people must die, he can detach himself from the politics of it all and just be with himself, above it all, doing his duty as a soldier. The speaker looking at the swans admires their beauty. However, he seems depressed and lonely. Perhaps if he had more energy and a sense of adventure like the airman he wouldn't sound so miserable and unhappy. Maybe his life would feel more worthwhile.

My second reason is that in both poems, Yeats uses a rhyming scheme but 'An Irish Airman Foresees His Death' has a great rhythm or beat to it also. Each line has eight syllables and the way the words sound reminds me of a plane floating and balancing in the air. The final line is a great example of this: 'In balance with this life, this death' creates an image of a small, fragile plane wobbling and balancing through the 'tumult' of the clouds above and I really like this. These are my two reasons for preferring this poem even though both are very good.

(346 words)

EXAMINER'S ASSESSMENT

The candidate shows a very good grasp of the preferred poem. Given that it is not the one on the page, this is to be commended. The candidate chooses two **specific reasons** for the preference and provides quotation to back up their views. There is clarity especially where the candidate takes a dim view of the speaker in the other poem: taking this **personal view** and providing some back-up with quotation is indicative of a student who has engaged well with the task.

A very good response overall.

MARKS AWARDED

12 (P+C) + 8 (L+M) = 20/20 (O1 Grade)

9 Time-keeping and Revision Checklist

aims
- To learn an efficient **time schedule** for the exam papers.
- To develop an effective **checklist for revision**.

Time schedule for the exam

Students frequently wonder how much they should write in the exam. Rather than thinking in terms of lines or pages, a better question is: **how much can I write in the time allowed?** If the Comprehension B question should take 35 minutes, consider how much you can plan and write in that time. The only real way to find out is to practise answers yourself. Follow the suggested outline below. It takes you through both papers chronologically to show you how your time should be divided.

exam focus

These times are approximate. The goal is to answer the questions as best you can in the time allowed.

Paper 1: Wednesday morning

9.30 a.m.	Begin by reading the entire paper – slowly. Take 10 minutes to read and choose your questions.
9.40 a.m.	Comprehension A (1, 2, 3) carries 50 marks. Allow 35 minutes.
10.15 a.m.	Begin Comprehension B. It carries 50 marks, so allow 35 minutes. Take 5 minutes to plan your piece and 30 minutes to write it.

10.50 a.m. Begin your Composition plan. Think broadly and try to get your opening and conclusion sorted first. Take 10 minutes to plan your composition.

11.00 a.m. Start the Composition. It carries 100 marks. You now have 80 minutes to finish the exam. You should use 10 of these 80 minutes to go back over your work. Do not leave early unless you are totally satisfied with your efforts.

12.20 p.m. Paper 1 ends.

After Paper 1 you should rest, rest, rest!

Paper 2: Thursday afternoon

2.00 p.m. Begin by quickly indentifying your: Single Text (one out of nine); preferred Comparative mode (one out of two); and preferred Poem (one out of four). Read only the questions relevant to your chosen texts. Mark them clearly on your exam paper. Allow 10 minutes for all of this.

> **The exam is not a sprint! There are no marks for finishing early.**

2.10 p.m. Single Text Question 1 (a, b and c). There are 30 marks here, so allow 30 minutes.

2.40 p.m. Single Text Question 2. There are 30 marks here, so allow 25 minutes. Make a short plan to help you answer this question.

3.05 p.m. Comparative Study. There are two questions: one with 30 marks and another with 40 marks. Aim to write more on the second question. Allow 65 minutes in total.

4.10 p.m. Unseen Poetry. Read the poem slowly at least three times. Pause. Answer the two 10-mark questions. Write quickly here. You have only 20 minutes.

4.30 p.m. Prescribed Poetry. Read your chosen poem twice. You now have 50 minutes to finish the exam. Answer the Prescribed Poetry questions in 45 minutes and leave yourself 5 minutes at the end to look back at your answers.

> **Time always flies in exam situations, so don't dwell too much on your work. Check over everything once at the end of the exam.**

5.20 p.m. English Leaving Certificate exam ends.

Revision checklist

Refer to the checklists below in preparation for your exam. Relevant chapters are listed as a reminder.

Paper 1 Checklist

- Different **Language Genres**: See Chapters 2, 3, 4 and 5.
  - Informative language
  - Narrative language
  - Persuasive language
  - Argumentative language
  - Aesthetic language
- Two basic writing **styles** (and their variations): See Chapters 4 and 5.
  - Story
  - Discussion
- Do you prefer telling stories or having discussions? See Chapter 5.
- Do you understand the difference between a story and a personal essay? See Chapter 5.

Paper 2 Checklist

- The name and correct spelling of the **title** and **author** of your **Single Text**. See Chapter 6.
- The **storyline** of your Single Text. You must know this in great detail. See Chapter 6.
- The main **characters** of your Single Text and their major **traits**. See Chapter 6.
- The **major themes** or issues raised by your Single Text. See Chapter 6.
- The names and correct spellings of the **texts** for your **Comparative Study**. See Chapter 7.
- Your favourite or 'anchor' **text** for the Comparative Study. Also, your least favourite, if you have studied three. See Chapter 7.
- The three **modes** for the Comparative Study. See Chapter 7.
- The **key moments** in your chosen Comparative Texts. See Chapter 7.
- The twelve most important **terms** in poetry. See Chapter 8.
- The value of understanding **feelings** in poetry and being able to write about them in your answers. See Chapter 8.

General checklist

- The length of **time** that you can spend on each section of the exam. See the time guide above.
- The **length** that you expect your answers to be (in terms of pages or paragraphs).
- The importance of **structure** in your exam answers. Compositions will have defined features, as suggested in the questions. Paper 2 answers should follow the formula: **point–quote–support**.
- **Spelling and mechanics** count for **10 per cent** of all marks. See the marking scheme in Chapter 2.
- **Sixty per cent** of the marks is for **what** you write and **40 per cent** is for **how** you write it. See the marking scheme in Chapter 2.
- Remember: exam success is mostly about **preparation**, with a little **perspiration** and some **inspiration** on the day!

If you are sure of all of the above, then you are well prepared for the Leaving Certificate English exam. However, a final word of warning: even the most seasoned English teacher will tell you that a certain amount of the exam is determined by the inspiration that a student experiences on the day. This cannot be taught. So, prepare well and do lots of work; then hope things go your way on the day!

Each student must do their very best with what they bring to the exam. The bottom line is to trust in your own ability. Generally, when you have worked really hard, you do reap rewards on the day of the exam.

Good luck!

Below is a glossary of useful words and phrases, many of which appear throughout this book.

Aesthetics are associated with beauty. Aesthetics are an essential aspect of creative writing.

Alliteration occurs when words that begin with the same letter are used close together for a sound effect.

Anchor text: This is the text that you know best from your Comparative Study. You will use this text as a base for your answers.

Argumentative language is logical language that aims to prove a point.

Atmosphere is a word used to describe the feelings generated by a piece of writing or suggested by a picture.

Audience: Those who experience a text or drama; people who will read your written work.

Bias is the state of favouring one side or having a strong preference.

Brainstorming is the process of jotting down all of your thoughts related to a specific issue.

Clarity means being clear and certain in your writing.

Cliché: A phrase that is tired, overused and lacks originality.

Climax is the moment of highest tension in a text, film or drama.

Coherence means making logical sense from beginning to end.

Commentary is writing that comments on or gives an opinion about some other work. See the Examiner's Assessments on Sample Answers throughout the text.

Composition: This is the second section of Paper 1; a piece of written work composed by a writer.

Comprehension means 'understanding'. Also, it is the name of the first question on Paper 1. It tests your ability to respond to questions on a given text extract.

Confidence is the sum total of one's feeling about oneself. Having confidence means having belief in one's abilities.

Diary: A day-to-day, informal or personal account of events. It is usually in written form.

Discussion: To have a discussion means to talk about an issue, to declare an opinion and to share it. Discussion appears throughout the book.

Emotive language is language that gives rise to emotions and strong reactions.

Format means the form that a piece of writing takes, what it looks like and how it is structured. Examination of format appears throughout the book.

Genre means a type of work. Texts can be classified into different genres, e.g. comedy, tragedy, horror.

Hero: The main character in a text. Sometimes heroes have a fatal flaw or weakness (hubris) that brings about personal tragedy.

Heroine: This is a female hero.

Hyperbole is gross exaggeration or overstatement.

Imagery means pictures generated in the mind by the written word.

Informative language is language that gives factual information.

Mechanics: The mechanics of language include spelling, grammar and punctuation. Mechanics are discussed throughout the book.

Metaphor is a colourful, creative description that is not to be understood literally. Metaphors are often found in poetry.

Metre is the beat or rhythm in a line of poetry.

Modes of Comparison are the headings under which you must compare texts in the Comparative Study.

Mood is the feeling generated by a text.

Narrative language is language used to tell a story.

Objective: An objective is something to aim for. 'Objective' has another meaning: to be objective means to be unbiased, to see things from all sides. The word 'objective' appears throughout the text.

Onomatopoeia occurs when the meaning of the word closely matches its sound, e.g. fizz, pop, crunch.

Personification occurs when non-human or inanimate objects are described as if they had human characteristics.

Persuasive language is language that tries to convince an audience of a particular viewpoint.

Planning is a vital aspect of writing any answer. Learn the art of being prepared! The notion of planning appears throughout the text.

Pun: This is a play on words. It occurs when words can be understood in more than one way.

Purpose is the reason behind something. You must always have a clear purpose when you are writing. Purpose appears throughout the book.

Quotation: The exact spoken words of a character in a text. Quotation appears throughout the text.

Register is a mixture of tone, vocabulary and purpose. Register is a vital characteristic that determines the success of your writing.

Relationships are an essential ingredient in all texts. Consider how people interact with each other in any text you study.

Resolution is the ending of a text.

Rhetorical question: This occurs when a question is asked and the answer is not given because it is either obvious or the questioner wants the audience to think and reflect.

Rhyme occurs when words that have similar sounds are used together for poetic effect.

Sarcasm is a scornful tone in writing and acting that pokes fun and can injure feelings.

Simile is a comparison that uses 'as' or 'like' to make a description more colourful.

Slang is low and somewhat vulgar forms of expression.

Social setting is the time and place in which a text is located.

Stanza is a collection of lines of poetry.

Statement is something written or spoken and usually presented as fact. Statements appear throughout the book.

Structure is how paragraphs and essays are shaped and put together. Structure is discussed throughout the book.

Syntax is the order in which words appear in a sentence.

Tension is a build-up of uncertainty, excitement or fear during a text.

Theme is the main issue raised or discussed by a text. It is more than just the plot or story.

Tone is the 'sound' of writing and the feeling suggested in its delivery. Tone creates a mood.

Verbiage is excessive language use, or writing that tries to sound sophisticated but isn't.

Verbose: To be verbose is to overuse language and sophisticated vocabulary that actually carries little genuine meaning.

Villain: The 'bad guy' in a text. Villains can be male or female.

Visuals are pictures, photographs, film stills, etc.

Vocabulary is a person's choice of words or level of language. Vocabulary is mentioned throughout the book.

Waffle is words that do not mean very much in the context of an exam answer.